# Goodbye

# Refined

# Sugar!

# Madame Labriski

**75+ RECIPES FOR BREAKFASTS AND SNACKS**

**DAIRY- GLUTEN- AND NUT-FREE OPTIONS**

# Goodbye Refined Sugar!

## EASY RECIPES WITH NO ADDED SUGAR OR FAT

madamelabriski.com

appetite

by RANDOM HOUSE

Appetite by Random House® and colophon are registered trademarks of Penguin Random House LLC.

Library and Archives of Canada Cataloguing in Publication is available upon request.

ISBN: 978-0-525-61081-6
eBook ISBN: 978-0-525-61082-3

Cover design: Talia Abramson
Interior design: Five Seventeen
Cover and book photography: Catherine Côté
Translated by Marie Asselin

Printed in China

Published in Canada by Appetite by Random House®,
a division of Penguin Random House Canada Limited.

www.penguinrandomhouse.ca

10 9 8 7 6 5 4 3 2 1

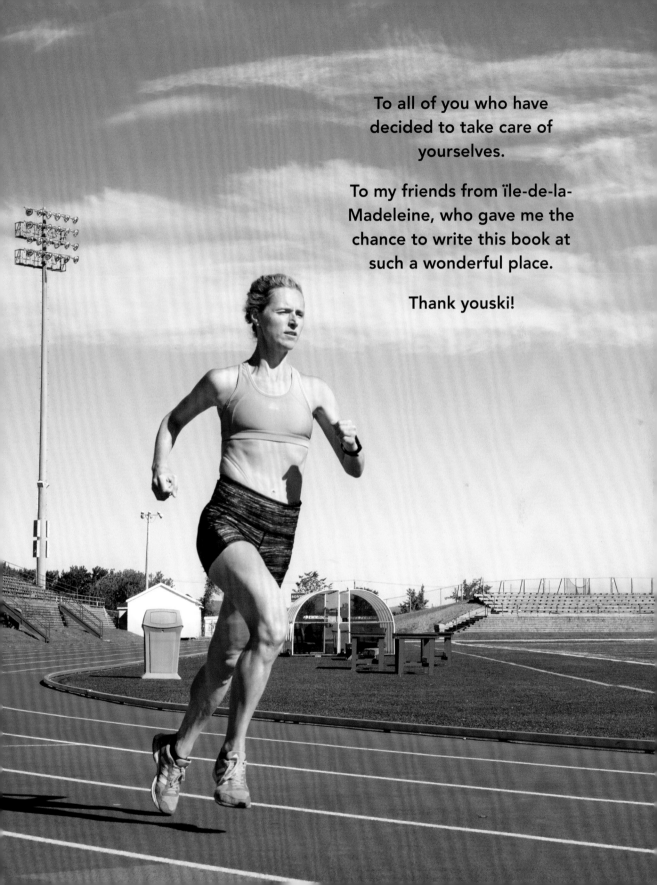

To all of you who have decided to take care of yourselves.

To my friends from île-de-la-Madeleine, who gave me the chance to write this book at such a wonderful place.

Thank youski!

# Table of Contents

# Foreword

I must admit, I have fallen in love with the Madame Labriski phenomenon. Apparently, I'm not the only one either: more than 130,000 people bought *Ces galettes dont tout le monde parle*—the French edition of *Fuel Your Day!*—in Quebec alone. I am extremely pleased that Madame Labriski is continuing her adventure with this second book. I am sure that you too will be delighted to discover her new recipes. You will also be happy to reconnect with her unique approach: easy recipes that use real food as ingredients, make you want to bake more often, and most important of all, are totally delicious!

You may be surprised to learn that, despite being a nutritionist, I have never calculated the nutritional value of Madame Labriski's recipes. This is probably because I don't need to do any calculations to know that, from a nutritional point of view, her recipes are excellent. What's more, I find that we are sometimes a little too bombarded with information on the amount of calories and nutrients found in our food. All of this information can make us lose our natural hunger cues. It's a shame to think that certain people decide to eat certain foods solely on the basis of their caloric content, instead of relying on their hunger and their desire to eat one food rather than another. Madame Labriski doesn't distract us with calories; we choose the recipes that appeal to us, we find our favorites, and we eat the little gems that we cooked up to fill our hunger and give us energy. However, in this book, Madame Labriski makes a notable exception for the Empowering Protein section (page 93), in which fiber, carbohydrate, and protein contents are indicated for athletes who need to put some fuel in their tank. This information may also be useful for people with diabetes who need to calculate the amount of carbohydrates in their diet.

You will see here, just as in her previous book, that pleasure is present in all its forms, with colorful recipe names and a presentation that highlights the taste, smell, and appearance of her energy treats. In short, Madame Labriski puts pleasure front and center. As a nutrition researcher, I strongly believe that we should make more use of such desires to promote healthy eating. Too often, I find that we seem to reserve our cravings for "forbidden" foods, which means we don't usually associate healthy foods and eating behaviors with great pleasure. Madame Labriski, with her bowl, her wooden spoon, and her good mood, contributes in a unique way to reconciling pleasure and healthy eating, and I thank her for it!

**Simone Lemieux, RD, PhD**
Professor, Laval University School of Nutrition
Researcher, Institute on Nutrition and Functional Foods

# Introduction

## Bonjour and welcome to the delicious, healthy, and fun world of Madame Labriski!

I'm fueled by my energy treats and want to change the world by saying goodbye to refined sugar! But first, let me take a step back . . .

Although I'm not a nutritionist or a pastry chef, I decided to pursue a crazy idea: to show that eating healthy can taste good *and* improve energy. So I tinkered in the kitchen and created my *pièce de résistance* (as they say): a healthy and nutritious date puree to use in place of refined sugar. Lo and behold, I was able to make healthy and yummy energy cookies, bites, bars, and more. And just like that, Madame Labriski was born. I launched my site madamelabriski.com and wrote my first book (my yellow book) called *Ces galettes dont tout le monde parle*, which was translated and adapted into *Fuel Your Day!* I also began to host various health and fitness events throughout my community, from wellness conferences to races, and sell packaged date puree, energy cookies, pancakes, and muffins throughout Quebec. It's been so exciting!

Then I began to think bigger. What if I could turn this idea into a movement and reduce the consumption of refined sugar once and for all? But how? I had a vision: to change the world one spoonful of date puree and one energy treat at a time. And so, I am back with even more recipes. That's right! Enjoy fortifying breakfast recipes, like The Maca Morning (page 18); even more energy cookies to transform your kids' lunches, such as The Fruity Study (page 49); nutritious muffins for that afternoon snack (I looooove The BettyBeet (page 73)); healthy protein-filled drinks, including The Purple Nitrat-o-Max (page 88); protein-packed goodies perfect for your pre- and post-workouts, The Log-Your-Results (page 98) go-to; and scrumptious desserts of all kinds, think The Applelicious Crisp (page 160), The Date Barski squares (page 159), or The Picky Logger Yule log for the holidays (page 153). I even have you covered with my recipes for healthy loaves (page 35–36) and biscotti (page 123–132)—or as I like to call them, Labriskotti! This book is also packed with helpful tips—or Tipskis!—and informative tidbits to help with your adventures in the kitchen.

I think that anything is possible . . . all you need is to believe and have confidence in yourself. Oh, and energize your day with healthy and fun treatskis! So go ahead and turn the page (and the next page, and the next . . . Ha! Ha!) to transform your kitchen, enjoy yummy and nutritious energy treats, and say goodbye to refined sugar once and for all!

*Madeerre Labroski*

# Do what you love. You will have all the energy in the world to realize your dreams.

These healthy recipes are as simple as boiling an egg. Now go grab your wooden spoon!

# Madame Labriski's Kitchen Essentials

**1 Scale!**
A scale saves time. Weighing while cooking ensures precision. I like that.

**2 Ice-Cream and Cookie Scoops!**
Ice-cream and cookie scoops add elegance to your culinary talent. How magnificent!

**3 Baking Sheets and Pans!**
Baking sheets and pans are sold in dollar stores (for only a buck or two!) and are perfect to get started. Treat yourself!

**4 Donut Mold!**
My indulgence for the year: a donut mold. For $10, my whole family goes completely nuts . . . we are crazy in love with it!

**5 Mini Nut Chopper!**
How magical! A mini nut chopper makes it possible to turn all nuts and seeds into flour.

**6 Silicone Mat!**
A silicone mat is super-essential! Don't walk; run and get yourself one. Nothing sticks to it.

**7 Wooden Spoon!**
A simple wooden spoon is ideal for mixing dough. It's so solid!

**8 Hand Blender!**
Forget futuristic machines! A simple hand blender is all you need.

# A Few Recipe Notes

## In the kitchen just as in life,
## you have tremendous potential.

The recipes found in this book follow a simple and tasty formula: date puree + unsweetened applesauce or yogurt + flavors of your choice = YUM! So this means you can get creative and tailor the recipe based on your needs. Are you looking for a recipe to satisfy a specific dietary requirement? No problem! Just use the icons below to find the recipe that's right for you.

### Icon Legend:

 Vegan

 Peanut- and nut-free

 Gluten-free

 Protein-packed

 Dairy-free

### *Also, keep an eye out for:*

- Tipski! Tips and tricks are always helpful in the kitchen.
- The Madame Labriski icon for those recipes that I love, love, loveski!
- And Madame's Menu, for ideas on how to take these recipes up a notch!

# Speaking of Tipskis, here are some helpful notes and answers to some frequently asked questions.

### Why date puree (page 11)?

Rich in fiber, dates have a neutral taste and fill you up with sustained energy: that's the magical secret of Madame Labriski!

### Are all of the recipes in this book really sweetened with date puree?

Yes. The base of each recipe is sweetened with date puree. But, some do suggest chocolate or caramel chips for a little extra love (it's okay to indulge sometimes. . . especially when the recipe is 100% free of refined sugar to begin with!).

### If I don't want to add chocolate or caramel chips, what should I do?

Just use seeds or dried fruit with no added sugar in its place.

### Do all of the recipes taste like dates?

Nope. A recipe will taste like dates only if it contains chopped dates.

### Can I make these recipes with any type of milk?

I specify plant-based milk or milk of your choice throughout. Whether it's almond, soy, or cow, use what feels right for you! I cow-dn't tell you otherwise, could I? Ha! Ha! Ha!

### What can I use as an egg substitute?

It's easy, and there are a few options. Choose the best for you!

- 1 tablespoon (15 ml) ground chia seeds + 3 tablespoons (45 ml) water
- 2 tablespoons (30 ml) ground flaxseeds + 2 tablespoons (30 ml) water
- ½ banana, mashed with a fork

### Can I substitute applesauce with yogurt?
Yes. Always.

### What about chia seeds and flaxseeds? Are they interchangeable?
Yep, they are. Always.

### What if I am allergic to almonds?
No problem! Grind your favorite seeds (pumpkin, sunflower, and so on) and substitute them for almond flour in any recipe that uses it.

### What else can I use instead of almond flour?
Organic tigernut powder is great! Tigernut is a surprising tuberous root that provides the same texture as almonds. It's available at your local health food store. You can also use any flour of your choice.

### What is organic maca powder?
Maca is a superfood that boosts energy levels in a stable, sustainable manner. You can get it at your local health food store.

### I have cricket powder on hand. Can I add it to your recipes?
Yes, you can add 2 to 3 tablespoons (30 to 45 ml) cricket powder to any recipe. Never heard of cricket powder? It is full of protein and very healthy for you (and is environmentally friendly). Oh, and it is available at health food stores.

### Your recipes include chocolate chips, white chocolate chips, etc. What if I want the recipe to be dairy-free?
Simply use dairy-free chocolate chips instead! I have marked the recipes where this dairy-free option is available.

### I have a convection oven. Do I need to modify the cooking times?
Slightly. Set your oven temperature to 325°F (160°C) instead of 350°F (180°C) and bake for the same amount of time directed by the recipes.

## Take care of yourself. Eat well.

# Goodbye Refined Sugar . . .

I have a sweet tooth, and I like to feast.
As a runner, I can feel famished.
And when I'm that hungry, I could eat an elephant!

Since I take care of myself, I don't want to eat just anything.
I want the best.
Bring me my food taster! Ha!

I have a sweet tooth, and I demand quality.
Not the unhealthy packaged snacks and sweets.
Empty calories . . . they're meaningless, right?
Why are so many popular recipes still in the Stone Age?

I'm not saying that you shouldn't eat any refined sugar . . .
Just that we eat too much.
And we don't have to.
We can fuel our day with date puree.

We need to change our eating habits now for the future.
I've got an idea, let's all do it together.
And say goodbye to refined sugar!

# . . . Hello Date Puree!

In life, we need sugar.
It's refined sugar that we need to eliminate.
Hello, date puree.
You make my life sweeter.

Yes, at your core you're a fruit.
You're a sugar, but a natural sugar, rich in fiber.
You're naturally sweet and have a neutral taste.
You're delicious and comforting.

I love you because you're full of goodness.
You feed me with so much energy.
You have this power to keep me going and going and going . . .
You fuel my day.

I love you in yogurt, an energy cookie, a tasty cake.
Or just by the spoonful.
Oh, the possibilities are endless.

Thanks to you, we can all feel vital and healthful.
And say goodbye to refined sugar.
Oh date puree, thank you for fueling our day!

# So How Do You Make Date Puree?

Date puree is at the heart of every recipe in this book. And making it is really easy!

**MAKES** 2½ cups (750 g)   **COOKING TIME**: 8 minutes

3 cups (500 g) pitted dates, chopped into pieces
1⅔ cups (410 ml) water

### And then what?

1   In a saucepan, bring the dates and water to a boil and simmer on medium heat until they're very soft, about 8 minutes. Stir and set aside.
2   Blend everything with a hand blender (zoom, zoom!) until you reach a texture similar to Greek yogurt. If you don't have a hand blender, simply stir vigorously with a spoon.
3   That's it!

**TIPSKI!**

Dates are sticky. Using kitchen shears to cut them makes things easier.

**TIPSKI!**

Date puree keeps refrigerated for 2 weeks in an airtight container. You can even freeze it. Yepski!

# 1
# Fortifying Breakfasts

*An energizing breakfast gives you wings!*

# The Madness Spreads

Empty calories to start the day? No thank you! These three spreads are so tasty and filling. So much so that my children think they are having a sugary treat! But shhhh! Don't tell them!

**MAKES** 1¼ cups (300 g) each
**OVEN TEMPERATURE:** 350°F (180°C)
**COOKING TIME:** 15 minutes

TIPSKI!

The spreads keep refrigerated for 2 weeks in an airtight container.

## The Hazella
*(hazelnut and cocoa spread)*

▎ 1 cup (130 g) unsalted whole hazelnuts

▎ ½ cup (150 g) date puree
▎ ¼ cup (25 g) cocoa powder

## The Caramellosel
*(cashew nut and caramel spread)*

▎ 1 cup (130 g) raw cashew nuts

▎ ½ cup (150 g) date puree
▎ ½ to 1 tablespoon (7 to 15 ml) artificial caramel extract, to taste
▎ ⅛ teaspoon (0.5 ml) fleur de sel

## The Café Crunch
*(coffee and almond spread)*

▎ 1 cup (130 g) unsalted whole almonds

▎ ½ cup (150 g) date puree
▎ 3 tablespoons (45 ml) espresso or 1½ tablespoons (22 ml) instant coffee powder

### And then what?

1   Preheat the oven to 350°F (180°C).
2   Spread the nuts from the orange section of the desired recipe on a baking sheet, then toast in the oven for 15 minutes.
3   If desired, rub the nuts against one another to remove the papery skin.
4   In a food processor or a mini chopper, grind the nuts finely.
5   Transfer the ground nuts to a bowl. Add the remaining ingredients from the blue section and mix well.
6   For a smoother consistency, add a bit of water and blend using a hand blender.
7   It's so good! How can you resist?!

# The Maca Morning

*(date, maca, and toasted coconut squares)*

A tasty, original, and stimulating recipe idea for your morning! That's what these energizing squares (or rectangles) are, and they complement your breakfast perfectly. Three, two, one . . . time to start your day!

**MAKES** 16 energy squares, about 2 inches (5 cm) each
**OVEN TEMPERATURE:** 350°F (180°C)   **COOKING TIME:** 20 minutes

½ cup (150 g) date puree

1 cup (250 ml) plant-based milk or milk of your choice

¼ cup (40 g) chia seeds

2 tablespoons (30 ml) raw maca powder (optional)

2 tablespoons (30 ml) raw cacao nibs

1 tablespoon (15 ml) cricket powder (optional)

1 cup (50 g) gluten-free corn flake cereal (I like Nature's Path Mesa Sunrise® Flakes)

½ cup (50 g) quinoa flakes or certified gluten-free quick-cooking oats

½ cup (75 g) chopped pitted dates

½ cup (25 g) toasted coconut flakes

¼ cup (35 g) shelled sunflower seeds

½ to 1 tablespoon (7 to 15 ml) artificial caramel extract (optional)

## And then what?

1   Preheat the oven to 350°F (180°C).

2   In a bowl, thoroughly combine all of the ingredients. That's it!

3   Line a square 8 inch (20 cm) baking pan with parchment paper or lightly grease—otherwise, everything will stick.

4   Pour the mixture into the prepared pan.

5   Bake for about 20 minutes.

6   Let cool to room temperature, then cut into 16 squares.

7   It's a great start to the morning!

### TIPSKI!

Did you know maca powder is natural and invigorating, and full of good things? It tastes like hazelnut and caramel.

**TIPSKI!**

The Friendly Scarlet
can also be enjoyed as
a dessert. It's great
with a scoop of
iced milk.

# The Friendly Scarlet

*(cherry and oat crumble)*

Cling, clang! Cling, clang! Add everything to the pan, bake, and then place the pan on the table. Watch out, though—it's hot . . . and especially good in your tummy. You'll smile all day when you add The Friendly Scarlet to your morning routine.

**MAKES** 4 to 6 servings, one 9 inch (23 cm) pie
**OVEN TEMPERATURE:** 350°F (180°C)   **COOKING TIME:** 28 minutes

1 tablespoon (15 ml) oil

2 tablespoons (30 ml) date puree

2½ cups (350 g) frozen dark sweet cherries

½ tablespoon (7 ml) cornstarch (optional)

½ cup (150 g) date puree

¼ cup (75 g) unsweetened applesauce

1 egg

2 teaspoons (10 ml) baking powder

2 tablespoons (30 ml) ground flaxseeds

½ cup (50 g) certified gluten-free oat flour or flour of your choice

½ cup (50 g) certified gluten-free rolled oats or regular rolled oats

Certified gluten-free rolled oats (optional)

## And then what?

1   Preheat the oven to 350°F (180°C).

2   Set an ovenproof 9 inch (23 cm) skillet over medium heat, then add all of the ingredients from the orange section.

3   Stir and simmer for about 8 minutes.

4   Meanwhile, prepare the crisp. In a bowl, combine all of the ingredients from the blue section.

5   Remove the skillet from the heat. Keeping the cherries in the skillet, spread the crisp overtop. If desired, sprinkle with additional rolled oats from the pink section.

6   Bake for about 20 minutes, then serve straight from the skillet.

7   It's official: this dish smells so fruity!

# The Golden French Toast

*(aka Labriski's French toast)*

French toast becomes a delicious masterpiece when dressed in a sweet coating made with date puree. What more could you ask for?

**MAKES** 4 slices    **STOVETOP TEMPERATURE:** Medium heat    **COOKING TIME:** A few minutes

⅓ cup (100 g) date puree

¼ cup (60 ml) plant-based milk
   or milk of your choice

1 egg

1 tablespoon (15 ml) chia seeds

1 tablespoon (15 ml) olive oil

4 slices of bread

Seasonal fruits, for serving

One of The Divine Delights (page 187),
   for serving

The Strawberry Thingy (page 184),
   for serving

## And then what?

1   To make the batter, in a bowl, combine all of the ingredients from the orange section.

2   Warm up the oil from the blue section in a skillet over medium heat.

3   Dunk a slice of bread from the pink section in the batter, then transfer to the skillet. Cook until golden brown; it will take a few minutes. Flip over and cook until golden brown on the second side, again just a few minutes.

4   Repeat to make all the French toasts.

5   Serve as desired using the toppings from the green section.

6   Your kitchen will smell delicious!

### MADAME'S MENU

**I love this with
The Healthy Chocolate
Sauce (page 187) and
fresh strawberries.**

# The Hola Quinoa!

*(warm quinoa cereal)*

Some warm quinoa to start your day? Why not! It's different and just so nourishing. What's more, you can prepare it in advance. Hello, endless energy—hola, quinoa!

**MAKES** 2 servings, ⅔ cup (150 g) each
**STOVETOP TEMPERATURE:** Medium heat  **COOKING TIME:** 10 to 15 minutes

½ cup (100 g) quinoa
⅓ cup (100 g) date puree
1 cup (250 ml) plant-based milk or milk of your choice, or water
1 tablespoon (15 ml) pure vanilla extract

½ tablespoon (7 ml) artificial caramel extract (optional)
½ to 1 tablespoon (7 to 15 ml) pumpkin spice extract (optional)

Berries, dried fruits, seeds, spices, coconut flakes, etc., for serving

## And then what?

1  Place the quinoa in a fine-mesh sieve, then rinse under cold running water.
2  Transfer the quinoa to a saucepan along with the ingredients from the orange section.
3  Add the other flavorings from the blue section if desired.
4  Bring to a simmer over medium-high heat, then lower the heat to medium-low and cook, uncovered, for 10 to 15 minutes, or according to the manufacturer's instructions. Quinoa is properly cooked when the grains are translucent and the white germs are visible around the grains.
5  Turn off the heat, cover, and let rest for about 5 minutes.
6  Add your choice of toppings from the pink section.

MADAME'S MENU

**The Hola Quinoa with fresh blueberries, sliced banana, shaved coconut, and pumpkin seeds is my go-to. It's so yummy!**

# The Unstoppable Granola

*(dried fruit, ginger, and maca granola)*

Madame Labriski granola? Yes. When granola contains no added sugar, the energy it provides is even better. Long live date puree! You'll feel unstoppable!

**MAKES** 4 cups (450 g)   **OVEN TEMPERATURE:** 350°F (180°C)   **COOKING TIME:** 24 minutes

¼ cup (75 g) date puree
⅓ cup (80 ml) plant-based milk or milk of your choice

2 tablespoons (30 ml) chia seeds
½ teaspoon (2 ml) ground ginger, or more to taste
2 tablespoons (30 ml) raw maca powder (optional)
2 tablespoons (30 ml) raw cacao nibs (optional)
Pinch of salt
1 cup (100 g) certified gluten-free rolled oats or regular rolled oats
¼ cup (50 g) gluten-free puffed cereal
½ cup (65 g) dried cranberries or raisins
½ cup (40 g) toasted coconut flakes
⅔ cup (113 g) mixed dried fruits (I like the Patience® Fruit & Co Organic Bursting Blend)

### And then what?

1   Preheat the oven to 350°F (180°C).
2   In a large bowl, combine the ingredients from the orange section.
3   Incorporate the ingredients from the blue section.
4   Line a baking sheet with parchment paper or lightly grease.
5   Spread the cereal on the baking sheet.
6   Bake for about 12 minutes, then stir and bake for another 12 minutes.
7   Turn the oven off and let the cereal rest in the oven's residual heat for at least an hour.
8   And here it is: an unstoppable granola.

### TIPSKI!

The granola will last in an airtight container at room temperature for 5 days. It's so, so good!

# Be confident and you can achieve anything!

# The Bomba Rosa Chia Pudding

*(cacao, raspberry, and coconut pudding)*

Surely, Madame Labriski didn't do this? Oh yes she did! After the success of The Bomba Rosa cookie found in *Fuel Your Day!*, here is an equally delicious chia pudding version. A good recipe is, after all, a good recipe.

**MAKES** 1 large serving or 2 smaller servings
**REFRIGERATION TIME:** 30 minutes

2 tablespoons (30 ml) date puree

1 cup (250 ml) plant-based milk or milk of your choice

¼ cup (40 g) chia seeds

2 tablespoons (30 ml) cacao powder

2 tablespoons (30 ml) certified gluten-free rolled oats or rinsed quinoa

⅔ cup (80 g) fresh or frozen raspberries

2 tablespoons (30 ml) toasted coconut flakes

1 to 2 tablespoons (15 to 30 ml) raw cacao nibs, to taste (optional)

## And then what?

1 In a bowl, thoroughly combine all of the ingredients.

2 Refrigerate for at least 30 minutes. That's it!

3 To serve, scoop into one or two bowls and garnish as desired.

TIPSKI!

For a more decadent chia pudding, sprinkle ¼ cup (50 g) chocolate chips over top.

# The Breakfast Buddha

*(breakfast roll filled with whatever you fancy)*

Wake up! It's time to make your life epic. Start the day with
these rolls to make you smile!

**MAKES** 1 log, 5 to 6 servings
**OVEN TEMPERATURE:** 350°F (180°C)   **COOKING TIME:** 25 minutes

¼ cup (75 g) date puree

1 cup (250 ml) plant-based milk or
milk of your choice

1 very ripe banana, mashed with a fork

2 tablespoons (30 ml) ground
flaxseeds

3 tablespoons (45 ml) goji berry
powder (optional)

¼ teaspoon (1 ml) ground cinnamon

Pinch of salt

1 cup (100 g) certified gluten-free
rolled oats or regular rolled oats

¼ cup (40 g) chia seeds

¼ cup (35 g) shelled hemp seeds

¼ cup (25 g) unsweetened shredded
coconut

One of The Divine Delights (page 187)
The Strawberry Thingy (page 184)

## And then what?

1   Preheat the oven to 350°F (180°C).
2   In a bowl, thoroughly combine all of the ingredients from the orange section. Yep, that's it!
3   Line a baking sheet with parchment paper.
4   Spread the dough over the baking sheet.
5   Bake for about 25 minutes.
6   Let cool for a few minutes.
7   Place a damp tea towel on your work surface.
8   Remove the cake from the baking sheet by lifting the parchment paper and turning the cake
over onto the towel. Peel the parchment paper
off the cake.
9   Working from the short side of the cake, roll
the cake, including the towel, into a log, then
let rest until cooled to room temperature.
10  Meanwhile, prepare the filling of your choice
from the blue section.
11  Once the cake is cool, unroll, remove the
towel, and spread the filling of your choice
over the cake. Ha! Ha! Ha!
12  Roll into a log again, then transform your log
into a Breakfast Buddha by cutting it into slices.

MADAME'S MENU

Filling The Breakfast
Buddha with some
Hazella (page 17) and
The Strawberry Thingy
(page 184) is a lovely
way to start
your day!

TIPSKI!

The Buddha slices can
be refrigerated in an
airtight container
for up to 1 week.

TIPSKI!

Did you know when finely ground, your favorite seeds and nuts transform into flours?

# The Alter and Go!

*(blueberry, sunflower seed, and quinoa loaf)*

This will be your new morning friend. A true symphony of freshness and flavors, it is also a good source of protein. It's official: power is in the air.

**MAKES** 1 loaf, 5 × 12 inches (13 × 30 cm)
**OVEN TEMPERATURE:** 350°F (180°C)   **COOKING TIME:** 1 hour, 10 minutes

½ cup (150 g) date puree

⅓ cup (100 g) unsweetened applesauce

1 egg

¾ cup (180 ml) water

1 tablespoon (15 ml) baking powder

Pinch of salt

½ cup (70 g) shelled sunflower seeds

½ cup (75 g) shelled and ground sunflower seeds

¼ cup (40 g) chia seeds

½ cup (50 g) certified gluten-free quick-cooking oats

½ cup (60 g) quinoa flour or flour of your choice

2 cups (280 g) fresh or frozen blueberries, or a combination of the two, lightly floured

Blueberries, for decoration

Shelled sunflower seeds, for decoration

## And then what?

1   Preheat the oven to 350°F (180°C).

2   In a bowl, thoroughly combine the ingredients from the orange section.

3   Add the ingredients from the blue section, wait for a light frothing to occur, then stir to combine.

4   Mix in the ingredients from the pink section.

5   Line a 5 × 12 inch (13 × 30 cm) loaf pan with parchment paper or lightly grease—otherwise, everything will stick.

6   Pour the mixture into the prepared pan, then decorate with the ingredients from the green section.

7   Bake for about 1 hour and 10 minutes.

8   While you wait, bask in the delightful aroma filling your kitchen.

9   Mamma mia, this is going to be good.

# The Natural and Powerful

*(date, sunflower seed, and hemp seed bread)*

Taking care of yourself has never been easier. Rich in fiber and protein, this breakfast bread is coming into your life on a silver platter. A great morning treat!

**MAKES** 1 breakfast loaf, 5 × 9 inches (13 × 23 cm)
**OVEN TEMPERATURE:** 350°F (180°C)  **COOKING TIME:** 45 minutes

½ cup (150 g) date puree

¾ cup (180 ml) plant-based milk or milk of your choice

1 egg

2 teaspoons (10 ml) baking powder

1 tablespoon (15 ml) pure vanilla extract

Pinch of salt

1½ cups (180 g) spelt flour or flour of your choice

½ cup (60 g) whole unsalted almonds

¼ cup (40 g) chia seeds

¼ cup (35 g) shelled hemp seeds

⅔ cup (110 g) pitted dates, chopped into pieces

⅔ cup (80 g) salted sunflower seeds

Pitted dates, for decoration (optional)

Shelled hemp seeds, for decoration (optional)

Shelled, salted sunflower seeds, for decoration (optional)

## And then what?

1   Preheat the oven to 350°F (180°C).

2   In a bowl, thoroughly combine all of the ingredients from the orange section. That's it!

3   Line a 5 × 9 inch (13 × 23 cm) loaf pan with parchment paper or lightly grease—otherwise, everything will stick.

4   Pour the batter into the prepared pan. If desired, decorate with the dates and seeds from the blue section.

5   Bake for about 45 minutes. Enjoy the sweet aroma coming from the oven.

6   Is this bread soft? No, but it's extremely nourishing.

### TIPSKI!

To fill yourself up with even more energy, top this bread with your favorite spread (page 16).

## TIPSKI!

You'll find packets of mixed dried fruits at the grocery store. If you can't find them, simply combine your favorite dried fruits. I like a mix of dried cranberries, blueberries, cherries, and goldenberries.

# The Rock Flower

*(almond and dried fruit pie)*

Treat yourself to a flower every morning. Enjoy a breakfast that is as healthful as it is quick to eat. A few mouthfuls and you will be rock solid. Go for it!

**MAKES** 6 servings, one 9 inch (23 cm) round pie
**OVEN TEMPERATURE:** 350°F (180°C)   **COOKING TIME:** 30 minutes

½ cup (150 g) date puree

¾ cup (180 ml) plant-based milk or milk of your choice

1 egg

2 teaspoons (10 ml) baking powder

½ tablespoon (7 ml) pure almond extract

¼ teaspoon (1 ml) ground cinnamon

2 tablespoons (30 ml) chia seeds

Pinch of salt

1 cup (120 g) gluten-free all-purpose flour or flour of your choice

½ cup (60 g) whole unsalted almonds

½ cup (60 g) shelled, salted pumpkin seeds

½ cup (65 g) raisins

⅔ cup (113 g) mixed dried fruits

Nuts of your choice, for decoration (optional)

Dried fruits, for decoration (optional)

## And then what?

1   Preheat the oven to 350°F (180°C).

2   In a bowl, thoroughly combine all of the ingredients from the orange section. That's it!

3   Line a 9 inch (23 cm) round pie or tart pan with parchment paper or lightly grease—otherwise, everything will stick.

4   Spread the mixture over the prepared pan. Decorate with nuts and/or dried fruits from the blue section if desired. Be creative and draw a flower with your ingredients!

5   Bake for about 30 minutes.

6   Try to let it cool before eating. (This isn't always easy.)

7   Ah! What a great start to the day!

# 2

# Energizing Cookies

*Happiness is an energy cookie that tastes like cloud nine.*

# The Vitavitality

*(matcha, raw cacao nib, and chocolate cookies)*

Oh, lush cookie, you make me feel alive and invigorated.
Thanks to you, I live my life with vitality. Ha! Ha! Ha!

**MAKES** 20 energy cookies, ½ ounce (15 g) each
**OVEN TEMPERATURE:** 350°F (180°C)   **COOKING TIME:** 10 minutes

¼ cup (75 g) date puree
¼ cup (75 g) unsweetened applesauce
1 egg

½ tablespoon (7 ml) baking powder
½ teaspoon (2 ml) baking soda
2 tablespoons (30 ml) matcha powder

½ cup (60 g) gluten-free all-purpose
flour or flour of your choice
¼ cup (35 g) raw cacao nibs
⅓ cup (17 g) unsweetened shredded
coconut
¼ cup (50 g) dairy-free dark chocolate
chips

Dark chocolate chips, for decoration

## And then what?

1   Preheat the oven to 350°F (180°C).
2   In a bowl, combine the ingredients from the
orange section.
3   Add the ingredients from the blue section.
Wait for a light frothing to occur, then mix well.
4   Stir in the ingredients from the pink section.
5   Line a baking sheet with parchment paper or
a silicone mat—otherwise, everything will stick.
6   Drop spoonfuls of dough using a small spoon
or cookie scoop to create beautifully round
energy cookies.
7   Decorate each cookie with a chocolate chip.
8   Bake for about 10 minutes. Transfer to a cooling
rack.
9   Add some green to your daily life with
The Vitavitality!

TIPSKI!

Did you know cacao nibs are rich in iron and fiber?

TIPSKI!

You can make this recipe using your favorite type of flour. Wowski!

# The Miss Veganette

*(oat, raisin, and non-allergenic cookies)*

A cousin of the famous The Miss Oatykins from *Fuel Your Day!*, this delicious version can be baked without eggs. Really? Yes, indeed. The Miss Veganette is a classic allergen-free oaty pleasure—perfect for lunch boxes!

**MAKES** 23 energy cookies, 1 ounce (30 g) each
**OVEN TEMPERATURE:** 350°F (180°C)   **COOKING TIME:** 15 minutes

½ cup (150 g) date puree

½ cup (150 g) unsweetened applesauce

¼ cup (60 ml) plant-based milk or milk of your choice

2 teaspoons (10 ml) pure vanilla extract

2 teaspoons (10 ml) baking powder

2 tablespoons (30 ml) chia seeds

1 tablespoon (15 ml) vinegar

½ tablespoon (7 ml) ground cinnamon

Pinch of salt

1 cup (100 g) certified gluten-free oat flour

1 cup (100 g) certified gluten-free quick-cooking oats

½ cup (65 g) raisins

Golden raisins, for decoration

## And then what?

1   Preheat the oven to 350°F (180°C).
2   In a bowl, thoroughly combine the ingredients from the orange section. Wow, it fizzles!
3   Add the ingredients from the blue section.
4   Line a baking sheet with parchment paper or a silicone mat—otherwise, everything will stick.
5   Drop spoonfuls of dough using a small spoon or cookie scoop to create beautifully round energy cookies.
6   Decorate each cookie with a few raisins.
7   Bake for about 15 minutes. Transfer to a cooling rack.
8   Enjoy the mouthwatering aroma . . . and give some to your friends who suffer from food intolerances or allergies.

# The Fiesta Grenada

*(strawberry, cranberry, and almond cookies)*

Spoil yourself with strawberries, see life through rose-colored glasses, and then dance for joy! That's life when you enjoy this deliciously mad snack. You will have craaaaaazy fun!

**MAKES** 25 energy cookies, 1 ounce (30 g) each
**OVEN TEMPERATURE:** 350°F (180°C)   **COOKING TIME:** 15 minutes

½ cup (150 g) date puree

½ cup (150 g) unsweetened apple-strawberry applesauce

2 teaspoons (10 ml) baking powder

1 packet (3.3 g) Pomegranate Cherry Crystal Light

Pinch of salt

1 cup (100 g) almond flour

½ cup (50 g) gluten-free flour or flour of your choice

½ cup (50 g) unsweetened shredded coconut

½ cup (65 g) dried cranberries

2 tablespoons (30 ml) chia seeds

8 to 10 (or more) fresh strawberries, sliced

½ cup (100 g) dairy-free white or dark chocolate chips (optional)

Halved strawberries, for decoration

## And then what?

1   Preheat the oven to 350°F (180°C).

2   In a bowl, thoroughly combine the ingredients from the orange section.

3   Add the ingredients from the blue section and mix well.

4   Line a baking sheet with parchment paper or a silicone mat—otherwise, everything will stick.

5   Drop spoonfuls of dough using a small spoon or cookie scoop to create beautifully round energy cookies.

6   Decorate each cookie with a slice of fresh strawberry.

7   Bake for about 15 minutes. Transfer to a cooling rack.

8   Hmm . . . it tastes red. Ha! Ha! Ha!

### TIPSKI!

Don't want to use Crystal Light? Add 1 tablespoon (15 ml) pure vanilla extract and a few drops of red food coloring.

# The Fruity Study

*(cranberry and hemp seed cookies)*

This cookie has serious character and it's extremely nourishing.
It also has a fruity lightness to it. It's top of the class all the way.

**MAKES** 17 energy cookies, 1 ounce (30 g) each
**OVEN TEMPERATURE:** 350°F (180°C)   **COOKING TIME:** 20 minutes

½ cup (150 g) date puree

½ cup (150 g) unsweetened applesauce

¼ cup (60 ml) plant-based milk or milk of your choice

2 teaspoons (10 ml) baking powder

1 tablespoon (15 ml) vinegar

2 tablespoons (30 ml) chia seeds

1 tablespoon (15 ml) pure vanilla extract

3 drops orange or lemon essential oil (optional)

Pinch of salt

½ cup (60 g) spelt flour

½ cup (50 g) rolled oats

¼ cup (35 g) shelled hemp seeds

½ cup (65 g) dried cranberries

Dried cranberries, for decoration

## And then what?

1   Preheat the oven to 350°F (180°C).
2   In a bowl, thoroughly combine the ingredients from the orange section. Wow, it fizzles!
3   Add the ingredients from the blue section.
4   Line a baking sheet with parchment paper or a silicone mat—otherwise, everything will stick.
5   Drop spoonfuls of dough using a small spoon or cookie scoop to create beautifully round energy cookies.
6   Decorate each cookie with a few dried cranberries.
7   Bake for about 20 minutes. Transfer to a cooling rack.
8   Health is serious business. Cook these cookies regularly.

**TIPSKI!**

For a perfect score on the health scale, use dried cranberries sweetened with apple juice.

# The Chocooh-La-La

*(crazy-for-chocolate cookies)*

Chocolate lovers, your mouth will burst with so much taste that you'll go head over heels for The Chocooh-La-La. As a bonus, these cookies are a source of fiber and chocolate. Tra-la-la-la!

**MAKES** 18 energy cookies, 1 ounce (30 g) each
**OVEN TEMPERATURE:** 350°F (180°C)   **COOKING TIME:** 15 minutes

½ cup (150 g) date puree

½ cup (150 g) unsweetened applesauce

¼ cup (60 ml) plant-based milk or milk of your choice

2 teaspoons (10 ml) pure vanilla extract

2 teaspoons (10 ml) baking powder

1 tablespoon (15 ml) vinegar

Pinch of salt

¾ cup (75 g) gluten-free flour or flour of your choice

½ cup (50 g) cacao powder

2 tablespoons (30 ml) chia seeds

½ cup (100 g) dairy-free dark chocolate chips

¼ cup (35 g) raw cacao nibs (optional)

¼ cup (25 g) unsweetened shredded coconut (optional)

Unsweetened shredded coconut, for decoration (optional)

## And then what?

1   Preheat the oven to 350°F (180°C).

2   In a bowl, thoroughly combine the ingredients from the orange section. Wow, it fizzles!

3   Add the ingredients from the blue section and mix well.

4   Line a baking sheet with parchment paper or a silicone mat—otherwise, everything will stick.

5   Drop spoonfuls of dough using a small spoon or cookie scoop to create beautifully round energy cookies.

6   Top with more shredded coconut from the pink section, if desired. Or just top half!

7   Bake for about 15 minutes. Transfer to a cooling rack.

8   Warning: the incredible smell of this delicious treat will fill you with joy.

You'll have fun making these healthy treats no matter how old you are. Age is only a number!

# The Angelico Mi Amor

*(hazelnut and Frangelico liqueur cookies)*

Festive and full of surprises, this cookie is sure to impress your guests. They will fall in love at the first bite. And is it healthy? It sure is!

**MAKES** 28 energy cookies, 1 ounce (30 g) each
**OVEN TEMPERATURE:** 350°F (180°C)   **COOKING TIME:** 15 minutes

½ cup (150 g) date puree

½ cup (150 g) unsweetened applesauce

1 egg

2 teaspoons (10 ml) baking powder

3 tablespoons (45 ml) Frangelico liqueur

3 tablespoons (45 ml) hazelnut-flavored instant coffee

1 cup (120 g) gluten-free all-purpose flour or flour of your choice

¼ cup (30 g) ground flaxseeds

¾ cup (70 g) chopped hazelnuts

¼ to ½ cup (50 to 100 g) dairy-free dark chocolate chips, to taste

Halved hazelnuts, for decoration

## And then what?

1   Preheat the oven to 350°F (180°C).
2   In a bowl, combine the ingredients from the orange section.
3   Add the ingredients from the blue section. Wait for a light frothing to occur, then mix well.
4   Incorporate the ingredients from the pink section.
5   Line a baking sheet with parchment paper or a silicone mat—otherwise, everything will stick.
6   Drop spoonfuls of dough using a small spoon or cookie scoop to create beautifully round energy cookies.
7   Decorate each cookie with a half hazelnut from the green section.
8   Bake for about 15 minutes. Transfer to a cooling rack.
9   Enjoy the tantalizing smell . . . and share with your friends!

# The Salted Psst-Psst-Pistachio

*(chocolate and pistachio cookies)*

With such a sing-songy name, this cookie is worthy of becoming the national anthem of pistachios. Sweet and salty, its texture is the epitome of perfection. It's time for pistachios!

**MAKES** 20 energy cookies, 1 ounce (30 g) each
**OVEN TEMPERATURE:** 350°F (180°C)   **COOKING TIME:** 15 minutes

½ cup (150 g) date puree

¼ cup (60 ml) plant-based milk or milk of your choice

1 egg

½ tablespoon (7 ml) baking powder

⅛ teaspoon (0.5 ml) fleur de sel

½ cup (60 g) gluten-free all-purpose flour or flour of your choice

¼ cup (30 g) coconut flour

½ cup (60 g) shelled pistachios (salted or unsalted)

½ cup (100 g) dairy-free chocolate chips

Dairy-free chocolate chips, for decoration (optional)

Shelled pistachios (salted or unsalted), for decoration (optional)

## And then what?

1   Preheat the oven to 350°F (180°C).

2   In a bowl, combine all of the ingredients from the orange section.

3   Line a baking sheet with parchment paper or a silicone mat—otherwise, everything will stick.

4   Drop spoonfuls of dough using a small spoon or cookie scoop to create beautifully round energy cookies.

5   Decorate each cookie with desired decorations from the blue section.

6   Bake for about 15 minutes. Transfer to a cooling rack.

7   I'm telling you, this is the cookie of the century. Ha! Ha! Ha!

### TIPSKI!

If you use dark chocolate chips, your happiness—just like the flavor—will be even more intense.

# The Cut-Me-Loose

*(cocoa and pecan cookies)*

Inspired by the famous Turtles™, this egg-free cookie recipe will be a powerful source for joy . . . now grab those cookie cutters!

**MAKES** 20 energy cookies in fun shapes, about ⅔ ounce (20 g) each
**OVEN TEMPERATURE:** 350°F (180°C)   **COOKING TIME:** 15 minutes

½ cup (150 g) date puree

¼ cup (75 g) unsweetened applesauce

1 tablespoon (15 ml) artificial caramel extract

2 tablespoons (30 ml) chia seeds

½ cup (55 g) pecan flour

¼ cup (25 g) cocoa powder

½ cup (60 g) gluten-free all-purpose flour or flour of your choice

About 2 tablespoons (30 ml) cocoa powder (to sprinkle over your work surface)

About 2 tablespoons (30 ml) pecan flour

About 2 tablespoons (30 ml) dairy-free chocolate chips, caramel toffee bits, or dairy-free caramel chips, divided

A few halved pecans to impress your guests (optional)

## And then what?

1   Preheat the oven to 350°F (180°C).

2   In a bowl, combine all of the cookie dough ingredients from the orange section and mix until a nice ball of dough forms. (Yum, yum! So delicious to snack on!)

3   Sprinkle a bit of cocoa powder over your work surface and on the palms of your hands—yes, yes, as a replacement for regular flour.

4   Transfer the dough to the prepared work surface and use a rolling pin to roll it to a ⅓ inch (1 cm) thickness.

5   Sprinkle the rolled dough with pecan flour and some chocolate chips. Gently press the garnishes into the dough.

6   Great! You can now use the cookie cutters to cut the dough into fun and creative shapes.

7   Decorate as desired with a half pecan and/or chips.

8   Line a baking sheet with parchment paper or a silicone mat—otherwise, everything will stick.

9   Bake for about 15 minutes. Transfer to a cooling rack.

10   Enjoy eating this sweet treat with your family!

# The Hazel-Filbert

*(chocolate, hazelnut, and quinoa square cookies)*

Believe it or not, filberts and hazelnuts are the same nut.
Are they really? Yep, they are! Really? Yes! Filbert = hazelnut.
Hazelnut = filbert.

And this is a square cookie? Why, yes! Ha! Ha! Ha!

**MAKES** 18 energy square cookies, 1 ounce (30 g) each
**OVEN TEMPERATURE:** 350°F (180°C)   **COOKING TIME:** 15 minutes

⅔ cup (200 g) date puree

1 egg

Generous pinch of salt

¼ cup (40 g) chia seeds

1 cup (100 g) quinoa flakes or certified
gluten-free quick-cooking oats

1 cup (100 g) ground hazelnuts

½ cup (100 g) dairy-free dark
chocolate chips

Dark chocolate chips, for decoration
(optional)

Halved hazelnuts, for decoration
(optional)

### And then what?

1   Preheat the oven to 350°F (180°C).

2   In a bowl, thoroughly combine the ingredients
from the orange section.

3   Line a baking sheet with parchment paper or
a silicone mat—otherwise, everything will stick.

4   Press the dough over the baking sheet down
to a 1 inch (2.5 cm) thickness.

5   Decorate as desired with dark chocolate chips
and/or halved hazelnuts.

6   Bake for about 15 minutes.

7   These cookie squares smell so good. The challenge is letting them cool a little before having
a taste. But I know you can do it!

TIPSKI!

Use a pizza cutter
to easily cut the
cookies.

# 3
# Pleasing Muffins

*There is joy in a fiber-rich muffin!*

# The Modern Financier

*(almond and grapefruit muffins)*

Normally financiers (delightful little French almond cakes) are shaped like gold bars. Since one needs to break convention sometimes, I thought it would be fun to cook them in a muffin pan instead. They are so rewarding!

**MAKES** 12 muffins   **OVEN TEMPERATURE:** 350°F (180°C)   **COOKING TIME:** 25 minutes

⅓ cup (100 g) date puree

4 egg whites or 2 whole eggs

1 teaspoon (5 ml) baking powder

3 tablespoons (45 ml) grapefruit zest

1 tablespoon (15 ml) grapefruit juice

1 cup (100 g) almond flour

½ cup (50 g) certified gluten-free oat flour

¼ cup (25 g) slivered almonds

Grapefruit zest, for decoration (optional)

Whole, skinned or slivered almonds, for decoration (optional)

### And then what?

1   Preheat the oven to 350°F (180°C).
2   In a bowl, thoroughly combine all of the ingredients from the orange section. That's it!
3   Line the muffin pan with parchment paper or silicone liners—otherwise, everything will stick.
4   Divide the batter evenly among the cups. If desired, decorate each muffin with additional zest and almonds from the blue section.
5   Bake for about 25 minutes.
6   These will help you amass a fortune… of joy and happiness in your mouth! Ha! Ha! Ha!

# The Pop Up Your Potential

*(almond butter and berry muffins)*

If you change the first three letters of "potential" you get "essential". . . and the potential taste in this muffin is essential for you. Wow! That's powerful. Just like this fruity delight.

**MAKES** 12 large muffins   **OVEN TEMPERATURE:** 350°F (180°C)   **COOKING TIME:** 25 minutes

½ cup (150 g) date puree

½ cup (150 g) natural almond butter

¼ cup (60 ml) plant-based milk or milk of your choice

1 egg

½ tablespoon (7 ml) baking powder

Pinch of salt

1 cup (120 g) gluten-free flour or flour of your choice

¼ cup (40 g) chia seeds

1 cup (140 g) frozen blueberries or (120 g) frozen raspberries (or ½ cup of each)

½ cup (60 g) dried blueberries

½ cup (50 g) almond flour

12 blueberries or raspberries (or half of each)

## And then what?

1   Preheat the oven to 350°F (180°C).

2   In a bowl, thoroughly combine the ingredients from the orange section.

3   Incorporate the ingredients from the blue section.

4   Line the muffin pan with parchment paper or silicone liners—otherwise, everything will stick.

5   Divide the batter evenly among the cups. Top each muffin with a berry from the pink section.

6   Bake for about 25 minutes.

7   Oh, that's good . . . so good, it's essential.

**TIPSKI!**

Allergic to nuts? No problem. You can make these muffins with nut-free peanut butter, like Wowbutter®.

# The Inspiring Coco-Banana

*(banana, coconut, and chocolate muffins)*

Dreamy texture. Perfect taste. It's like gluten-free haute cuisine worthy of the greatest chef . . . and today, that chef is you. So go—mix everything and taste your talented creation!

**MAKES** 10 large muffins   **OVEN TEMPERATURE:** 350°F (180°C)   **COOKING TIME:** 30 minutes

½ cup (150 g) date puree

2 bananas, mashed with a fork

⅔ cup (160 ml) plant-based milk or milk of your choice

1 egg

½ tablespoon (7 ml) baking powder

Pinch of salt

¾ cup (90 g) gluten-free flour or flour of your choice

¼ cup (30 g) coconut flour

¼ cup (40 g) chia seeds

¼ cup (13 g) unsweetened coconut flakes

¼ cup (50 g) dairy-free dark chocolate chips or dairy-free milk chocolate chips

Coconut flakes, for decoration

## And then what?

1   Preheat the oven to 350°F (180°C).

2   In a bowl, thoroughly combine the ingredients from the orange section.

3   Incorporate the ingredients from the blue section.

4   Line the muffin pan with parchment paper or silicone liners—otherwise, everything will stick.

5   Divide the batter evenly among the cups. Decorate each muffin with some coconut flakes from the pink section.

6   Bake for about 30 minutes.

7   Do you recognize that tantalizing smell? That's the smell of inspiration.

# The Iron Know-How

*(buckwheat and date muffins)*

Bang! Pow! Bing bang pow! This naturally gluten-free recipe is like an iron tornado. Bring out your know-how and show us who we're dealing with . . . in the kitchen. It will be incredible!

**MAKES** 12 muffins **OVEN TEMPERATURE:** 350°F (180°C) **COOKING TIME:** 30 minutes

½ cup (150 g) date puree

½ cup (125 ml) plant-based milk or milk of your choice

1 egg

½ tablespoon (7 ml) baking powder

1 tablespoon (15 ml) artificial caramel extract (optional)

Pinch of salt

1 cup (150 g) buckwheat flour

¼ cup (30 g) ground flaxseeds

½ cup (85 g) pitted dates, chopped into pieces

2 tablespoons (30 ml) sprouted buckwheat (optional)

6 pitted dates, halved, for decoration

## And then what?

1 Preheat the oven to 350°F (180°C).

2 In a bowl, thoroughly combine the ingredients from the orange section.

3 Incorporate the ingredients from the blue section.

4 Line the muffin pan with parchment paper or silicone liners—otherwise, everything will stick.

5 Divide the batter between the cups. Decorate each muffin with a piece of date from the pink section.

6 Bake for about 30 minutes.

TIPSKI!

Sprouted buckwheat adds allergen-free crunch. We like that.

# The BettyBeet

*(spiced raw beet powder and raisin muffins)*

This fall delight adds color and positive energy to those chilly mornings. Long live raw beetroot powder and all its healthy benefits.

**MAKES** 12 muffins   **OVEN TEMPERATURE:** 350°F (180°C)   **COOKING TIME:** 30 minutes

½ cup (150 g) date puree

1½ cups (375 ml) plant-based milk or milk of your choice

1 egg

½ tablespoon (7 ml) baking powder

½ to 1 teaspoon (2 to 5 ml) four-spice blend, to taste

Pinch of salt

1 cup (120 g) gluten-free flour or flour of your choice

⅓ cup (50 g) raw beet powder (dehydrated beets)

¼ cup (25 g) certified gluten-free rolled oats

¼ cup (30 g) ground flaxseeds

⅔ cup (90 g) dried currants

Certified gluten-free rolled oats, for decoration

## And then what?

1   Preheat the oven to 350°F (180°C).

2   In a bowl, thoroughly combine the ingredients from the orange section.

3   Incorporate the ingredients from the blue section.

4   Line the muffin pan with parchment paper or silicone liners—otherwise, everything will stick.

5   Divide the batter between the cups. Sprinkle each muffin with rolled oats from the pink section.

6   Bake for about 30 minutes.

7   Let the muffins cool and . . . eat with a smile!

**TIPSKI!**

Four-spice blend is a delicious mix of cinnamon, cloves, ginger, and nutmeg. You can buy it ready-made in grocery stores.

# The Vegan Lucky Day

*(zesty muffins)*

Are you out of eggs but have a burning desire to cook gluten-free muffins with an irresistible *je ne sais quoi*? Well, this is your lucky day.

**MAKES** 10 muffins   **OVEN TEMPERATURE:** 350°F (180°C)   **COOKING TIME:** 25 minutes

⅓ cup (100 g) date puree

½ cup (125 ml) plant-based milk or milk of your choice

1 tablespoon (15 ml) pure vanilla extract

½ tablespoon (7 ml) baking powder

½ tablespoon (7 ml) vinegar

½ cup (75 g) chickpea flour

½ cup (60 g) tapioca flour or cornstarch

½ cup (50 g) almond flour

2 to 3 drops citrus essential oil or 1 tablespoon (15 ml) citrus zest, for a flavor punch (optional)

Citrus zest, for decoration (optional)

## And then what?

1 Preheat the oven to 350°F (180°C).

2 In a bowl, thoroughly combine the ingredients from the orange section. Wow, it fizzles!

3 Incorporate the ingredients from the blue section.

4 Add the desired flavor punch from the pink section.

5 Line the muffin pan with parchment paper or silicone liners—otherwise, everything will stick.

6 Divide the batter evenly among the cups. If desired, decorate each muffin with additional citrus zest.

7 Bake for about 25 minutes.

**TIPSKI!**

Allergic to almonds? Remember, you can substitute tigernut powder or grind your favorite seeds.

# The My Vegan Valentine

*(chocolate and hazelnut muffins)*

The vegan chocolate base of this muffin will remind you of a certain delicious chocolate hazelnut spread. Some people might tell you that it tastes like nirvana, while others will applaud the fact that it's gluten-free. But never mind—love is in the air.

**MAKES** 10 muffins  **OVEN TEMPERATURE:** 350°F (180°C)  **COOKING TIME:** 25 minutes

⅔ cup (200 g) date puree

½ cup (125 ml) plant-based milk or milk of your choice

½ tablespoon (7 ml) baking powder

½ tablespoon (7 ml) vinegar

½ cup (75 g) chickpea flour or flour of your choice

½ cup (50 g) cocoa powder

½ cup (50 g) ground hazelnuts

½ cup (100 g) dairy-free dark chocolate chips

Dairy-free chocolate chips, for decoration (optional)

Whole hazelnuts, for decoration (optional)

## And then what?

1  Preheat the oven to 350°F (180°C).

2  In a bowl, thoroughly combine the ingredients from the orange section. Wow, it sizzles!

3  Incorporate the ingredients from the blue section.

4  Line the muffin pan with parchment paper or silicone liners—otherwise, everything will stick.

5  Divide the batter evenly among the cups and decorate each muffin with chocolate chips, if desired.

6  Bake for about 25 minutes.

7  It will certainly smell like loooooooove in the house when you make these!

TIPSKI!

You can turn all your nuts into powder using a coffee grinder. Have fun!

Work hard, play hard, have fun, and eat healthy! That's my recipe for success!

# The Goober-Peanuuuuuuts

*(oat and peanut muffins)*

Despite being delicious, this peanut muffin will never make it onto school grounds (but look at the Tipski for a nut-free variation!). It promises to be a favorite among your friends and family at home. It's time to treat yourself!

**MAKES** 12 large muffins or 36 mini muffins
**OVEN TEMPERATURE:** 350°F (180°C)   **COOKING TIME:** 25 to 35 minutes

½ cup (150 g) date puree

½ cup (150 g) natural peanut butter

¾ cup (180 ml) plant-based milk or milk of your choice

1 egg

½ tablespoon (7 ml) baking powder

Pinch of salt

½ cup (50 g) certified gluten-free quick-cooking oats

½ cup (100 g) finely ground peanuts (they should be close to a powdered texture)

¼ cup (40 g) chia seeds

Roughly chopped peanuts, for decoration

## And then what?

1   Preheat the oven to 350°F (180°C).

2   In a bowl, thoroughly combine all of the ingredients from the orange section. That's it!

3   Line the muffin pan with parchment paper or silicone liners—otherwise, everything will stick.

4   Divide the batter evenly among the cups. Sprinkle each muffin with the chopped peanuts from the blue section.

5   Bake the large muffins for 35 minutes or the small ones for 25 minutes.

6   Turn this recipe into the star of your snacks.

**TIPSKI!**

Remember, you can use Wowbutter® if there is a nut allergy. And in place of peanuts, you can use roasted soy nuts instead. Mmm!

# The My Heart Belongs to You Cranberry

*(holiday cranberry muffins)*

Biting into this tangy muffin reveals a hidden surprise!
Your heart will just love the cranberry.

**MAKES** 12 muffins   **OVEN TEMPERATURE:** 350°F (180°C)
**COOKING TIME:** 15 minutes (for The Saucy Cranberry) + 35 minutes

1½ cups (375 ml) The Saucy Cranberry
(page 183)

½ cup (150 g) date puree
½ cup (150 g) unsweetened
applesauce
½ cup (125 ml) plant-based milk or
milk of your choice
2 tablespoons (30 ml) chia seeds

½ tablespoon (7 ml) baking powder
½ tablespoon (7 ml) vinegar of your
choice
1¼ cups (150 g) spelt, whole wheat,
or gluten-free all-purpose flour
¾ cup (95 g) dried cranberries

## And then what?

1   Preheat the oven to 350°F (180°C).
2   Prepare The Saucy Cranberry (page 183).
3   In a bowl, thoroughly combine the ingredients
from the orange section.
4   Incorporate the ingredients from the blue
section.
5   Line the muffin pan with parchment paper or
silicone liners—otherwise, everything will stick.
6   Fill each cup halfway with the muffin batter.
Spoon some of The Saucy Cranberry in each
cup, then cover with more batter.
7   Bake for about 35 minutes.
8   It's beautiful, it's good, and it's chic!

**TIPSKI!**

Double-up on
The Saucy Cranberry
(page 183) to serve with
the muffins. Yummski!

# 4

# Surprising Beverages

*Surprising drinks that make you want to go above and beyond.*

# The Iced, Iced Matcha

*(matcha beverage)*

Fabulous. Perfect. I want more and more.

**MAKES** 1 cup (250 ml)

2 tablespoons (30 ml) date puree
1 cup (250 ml) plant-based milk
   or milk of your choice
2 teaspoons (10 ml) matcha powder
4 to 5 ice cubes

### And then what?

1   Place all of the ingredients in a
     blender, then blend until smooth.
2   Enjoy with a smile.

# The This Chocolate Is HOT!

*(cocoa powder beverage)*

Hot chocolate without added sugar? Ohhhhhhhhhh, yes—that hits the spot.

**MAKES** 1 cup (250 ml)   **COOKING TIME:** A few minutes

1 cup (250 ml) plant-based milk
   or milk of your choice
2 tablespoons (30 ml) date puree
1 tablespoon (15 ml) cocoa powder
⅛ teaspoon (0.5 ml) ground cinnamon
   (optional)

### *And then what?*

1   In a small pot over medium heat, heat the milk,
    stirring until just under boiling. Remove from
    the heat and allow it to cool for a few minutes.
2   Pour the hot milk and the rest of the ingredi-
    ents into a blender, then blend until smooth.
3   Take a big gulp of happiness . . . chocolate-
    flavored happiness.

# The Purple Nitrat-o-Max

*(blueberry and raw beet powder beverage)*

I like to enjoy simple things and being able to taste individual ingredients . . . except for raw beetroot powder, until now! Here is a drink rich in nitrates that won't "beet" up your taste buds. Get it?!

**MAKES** 1 cup (250 ml)

¼ cup (75 g) date puree

1 cup (140 g) frozen blueberries

1 cup (250 ml) plant-based milk
   or milk of your choice

½ to 1 tablespoon (7 to 15 ml) raw
   beet powder, to taste

¼ teaspoon (1 ml) matcha powder

## And then what?

1  Place all of the ingredients in a blender, then blend until smooth.
2  Relax and enjoy.

**TIPSKI!**

Want an invigorating sorbet? Make this recipe but cut the amount of liquid in half.

# The Red Gooooooji!

*(raspberry and goji berry powder beverage)*

Pureed dates in smoothies? That's right. Stir some into anything and every-thing. Just like goji berries—you'll see them more and more everywhere you go. It's a good thing goji berries are rich in antioxidants, isn't it?

**MAKES** 1 cup (250 ml)

¼ cup (75 g) date puree
1¼ cups (150 g) frozen raspberries
1 cup (250 ml) plant-based milk
    or milk of your choice
½ to 1 tablespoon (7 to 15 ml) goji
    berry powder, to taste

## And then what?

1   Place all of the ingredients in a
    blender, then blend until smooth.
2   Enjoy with love.

When life gets you down, take care of yourself, and don't forget to smile!

# 5

# Empowering Protein

*Long live proteins and long live having strength to spare!*

*This chapter includes nutritional information to meet the specific needs of athletes.*
*For recipes containing milk, the nutritional calculations were made using soy milk.*

# The Vanilla Muscle-Lix

*(protein-packed cereal)*

**Per Serving**

| | |
|---|---|
| Protein | **13 g** |
| Carbohydrates | **30 g** |
| Fiber | **5 g** |

After a workout, or just to get a rock-solid start to the day, these cereals deserve a gold medal. Enjoy!

**MAKES** 16 servings, ½ cup (55 g) each
**OVEN TEMPERATURE:** 350°F (180°C)  **COOKING TIME:** 24 minutes

¾ cup (225 g) date puree
¾ cup (180 ml) plant-based milk or milk of your choice
¼ cup (40 g) chia seeds
1 tablespoon (15 ml) to 1½ tablespoons (22 ml) pure vanilla extract

2½ cups (250 g) certified gluten-free rolled oats or regular rolled oats
2½ cups (48 g) gluten-free puffed cereal, or regular puffed cereal
1 cup (100 g) slivered almonds
⅓ cup (50 g) shelled hemp seeds
1 cup (120 g) shelled, salted pumpkin seeds
1 cup (120 g) chopped mixed dried fruits (blueberries, raisins, mangos, dates, etc.)

3 to 4 scoops (90 to 120 g) vanilla vegan protein powder (I like Vega® Protein & Greens Vanilla)

## And then what?

1  Preheat the oven to 350°F (180°C).
2  In a bowl, thoroughly combine the ingredients from the orange section.
3  Incorporate the ingredients from the blue section.
4  Line a baking sheet with parchment paper or lightly grease.
5  Spread the cereal over the baking sheet.
6  Bake for about 12 minutes, then stir and bake for another 12 minutes.
7  Turn the oven off and let the cereal rest in the oven's residual heat for at least an hour.
8  Take the cereal out, add the protein powder from the pink section, and mix well.
9  The granola will keep in an airtight container at room temperature for 5 days.

**TIPSKI!**

Served over Greek yogurt with chopped fresh fruit, this cereal is ideal to recover after exercise.

# The Triple Salto Brownie

*(plant protein and triple-chocolate brownie)*

**Per Serving\***

| | |
|---|---|
| Protein | **5 g** |
| Carbohydrates | **10 g** |
| Fiber | **2 g** |

*\*Includes optional ingredients*

This recipe is a cousin of the famous ChocoGo from *Fuel Your Day!* It took months of perseverance to create this dairy-free version. But if you put your mind to something . . . This is a crazily intense source of happiness.

**MAKES** 28 servings, 1 ounce (30 g) each
**OVEN TEMPERATURE:** 350°F (180°C)  **COOKING TIME:** 30 minutes

½ cup (150 g) date puree

1½ cups (375 ml) plant-based milk or milk of your choice

1 egg

½ tablespoon (7 ml) baking powder

Pinch of salt

½ cup (60 g) gluten-free all-purpose flour or flour of your choice

1 cup (100 g) powdered pea protein

½ cup (50 g) cocoa powder

½ cup (50 g) almond flour

½ to 1 cup (100 to 200 g) dairy-free dark chocolate chips, white chocolate chips, and/or milk chocolate chips

Dairy-free chocolate chips, for decoration (optional)

## And then what?

1   Preheat the oven to 350°F (180°C).

2   In a bowl, thoroughly combine all of the ingredients from the orange section.

3   Line a baking sheet with parchment paper or a silicone mat—otherwise, everything will stick.

4   Press the dough over the baking sheet down to a 1 inch (2.5 cm) thickness.

5   If desired, sprinkle with the chocolate chips from the blue section.

6   Bake for about 30 minutes.

7   Let cool, then use a pizza cutter to slice into 28 pieces of 1½ × 2 inches (4 × 5 cm) each.

8   And the aroma—how can I describe it? Three words: euphoria, joy, and applause.

# The Log-Your-Results

*(pea protein and whatever suits your fancy log)*

The Log-Your-Results is so tasty and melts in your mouth. I like to eat it before I go running early in the morning . . . I *woodn't* have it any other way.

**MAKES** 1 small log, 5 to 6 servings   **OVEN TEMPERATURE:** 350°F (180°C)   **COOKING TIME:** 20 minutes

½ cup (150 g) date puree

1 egg

1½ cups (375 ml) plant-based milk or milk of your choice

1 to 2 teaspoons (5 to 10 ml) baking powder

Pinch of salt

1 cup (100 g) powdered pea protein

½ cup (60 g) gluten-free all-purpose flour or spelt flour

Filling of your choice

**MADAME'S MENU**

**I loooooove to use Wowbutter® and The Strawberry Thingy (page 184) as fillings.**

## And then what?

1   Preheat the oven to 350°F (180°C).

2   In a bowl, thoroughly combine the ingredients from the orange section.

3   Incorporate the ingredients from the blue section, and then the ingredients from the pink section.

4   Line a baking sheet with parchment paper or lightly grease—otherwise, everything will stick.

5   On the prepared baking sheet, spread the dough in a rectangle 6½ inches (17 cm) long by ½ inch (1.5 cm) thick.

6   Bake for about 20 minutes.

7   Let cool for a few minutes.

8   Place a damp tea towel on your work surface.

9   Remove the cake by lifting the parchment paper out of the baking sheet. Turn the cake over onto the towel, then peel the parchment paper off the cake.

10   Working from the short side of the cake, roll the cake, including the towel, into a log, then let rest until cooled to room temperature.

11   Once the cake is cool, unroll, remove the towel, and spread the filling of your choice over the cake.

12   Roll into a log again without the towel.

13   To serve, cut into slices.

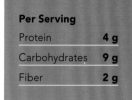

# The Goobaracha

*(oat, cricket, and powdered peanut butter cookies)*

Here's a cookie that's so energizing you will want to run your fastest or just sing and dance around your house. Ha! Ha!

**MAKES** 15 energy cookies, 1 ounce (30 g) each
**OVEN TEMPERATURE:** 350°F (180°C)   **COOKING TIME:** 15 minutes

⅓ cup (100 g) date puree

⅓ cup (80 ml) plant-based milk or milk of your choice

1 egg

1 tablespoon (15 ml) pure vanilla extract or artificial caramel extract

2 teaspoons (10 ml) baking powder

Pinch of salt

1 cup (100 g) certified gluten-free oat flour or flour of your choice

¼ cup (24 g) powdered peanut butter

¼ cup (24 g) cricket powder

2 tablespoons (30 ml) chia seeds

2 tablespoons (30 ml) shelled hemp seeds

¼ cup (50 g) dairy-free chocolate chips, peanut butter chips, or caramel chips

Shelled hemp seeds, for decoration (optional)

## And then what?

1   Preheat the oven to 350°F (180°C).

2   In a bowl, thoroughly combine the ingredients from the orange section.

3   Incorporate the ingredients from the blue section.

4   Line a baking sheet with parchment paper or a silicone mat—otherwise, everything will stick.

5   Drop spoonfuls of dough using a small spoon or cookie scoop to create beautifully round energy cookies. Decorate with more shelled hemp seeds from the pink section, if using.

6   Bake for about 15 minutes.

7   Go conquer your own sporting achievements. Goooooo!

### TIPSKI!

Powdered peanut butter is just that—peanut butter without its natural oils ground into a fine powder! You can buy it at the grocery store. Yummy!

**Per Serving**

| | |
|---|---|
| Protein | **2 g** |
| Carbohydrates | **7 g** |
| Fiber | **1 g** |

# The Pocket Bug

*(cricket and coffee protein balls)*

The taste of these crickets will remind you of a coffee-flavored chocolate bar. Put some in your pocket and go conquer those podiums.

**MAKES** 30 protein balls, ½ ounce (15 g) each
**OVEN TEMPERATURE:** 350°F (180°C)   **COOKING TIME:** 10 minutes

½ cup (150 g) date puree

½ cup (50 g) almond flour or tigernut powder

½ cup (60 g) soy protein powder

1 short espresso or 3 tablespoons (45 ml) filter coffee or 1 tablespoon (15 ml) instant coffee

10 to 20 pitted dates, diced, to taste

1 to 2 tablespoons (15 to 30 ml) cricket powder, to taste

½ tablespoon (7 ml) artificial caramel extract (optional)

Pinch of salt

¼ cup (25 g) almond flour (optional)

## And then what?

1   Preheat the oven to 350°F (180°C).

2   In a bowl, thoroughly combine the ingredients from the orange section. The dough should come together into a nice ball.

3   Lightly grease your hands (with vegetable oil, for example) before handling the dough.

4   Divide and roll the dough into 30 small balls. You can flatten them, if you prefer that shape.

5   If desired, roll the balls in the almond flour from the blue section.

6   Line a baking sheet with parchment paper or a silicone mat—otherwise, everything will stick.

7   Set your creations on the prepared baking sheet.

8   Bake for about 10 minutes. Enjoy.

### TIPSKI!

Eating two or three Pocket Bugs after training will turn you into a champ.

# The Green Pocket

*(almond matcha protein balls)*

**Per Serving**

| | |
|---|---|
| Protein | **2 g** |
| Carbohydrates | **4 g** |
| Fiber | **1 g** |

Pure energy in your pocket. After training, The Green Pocket has the power to fulfill you until your next meal . . . if it's not too far away. A zen solution.

**MAKES** 24 protein balls, ½ ounce (15 g) each
**OVEN TEMPERATURE:** 350°F (180°C)   **COOKING TIME:** 10 minutes

½ cup (150 g) date puree

½ cup (50 g) almond flour or tigernut powder

½ cup (60 g) soy protein powder

1 to 2 tablespoons (15 to 30 ml) matcha powder, to taste

Pinch of salt

¼ cup (25 g) almond flour, for decoration (optional)

1 tablespoon (15 ml) matcha powder, for decoration (optional)

## And then what?

1   Preheat the oven to 350°F (180°C).

2   In a bowl, thoroughly combine the ingredients from the orange section. The dough should come together into a nice ball.

3   Lightly grease your hands (with vegetable oil, for example) before handling the dough.

4   Divide and roll the dough into 24 small balls.

5   If desired, combine the ingredients from the blue section, then roll the balls in the coating.

6   Line a baking sheet with parchment paper or a silicone mat—otherwise, everything will stick.

7   Set your creations on the prepared baking sheet.

8   Bake for about 10 minutes. Time for the Green Pocket!

### TIPSKI!

**Having two or three Green Pockets after training will refuel you right up.**

Why eat foods that result in lower energy? That's why I choose pureed dates.

# The Soymazing

*(plant protein and peanut butter squares)*

**Per Serving**

| | |
|---|---|
| Protein | **11 g** |
| Carbohydrates | **17 g** |
| Fiber | **5 g** |

I'm crazy about peanut butter. To me, every bite tastes like determination. I also believe that positive visualization leads to victory.

**MAKES** 18 squares, 1¾ ounces (50 g) each
**OVEN TEMPERATURE:** 350°F (180°C)   **COOKING TIME:** 30 minutes

½ cup (150 g) date puree

½ cup (150 g) natural peanut butter

½ cup (125 ml) plant-based milk or milk of your choice

1 cup (100 g) certified gluten-free quick-cooking oats

1 cup (120 g) soy protein powder

¼ cup (40 g) chia seeds

¼ cup (35 g) shelled hemp seeds

1 cup (150 g) chopped peanuts (salted or unsalted)

½ cup (100 g) Reese's peanut butter chips

Chopped peanuts, for decoration (optional)

Reese's peanut butter chips, for decoration (optional)

## And then what?

1  Preheat the oven to 350°F (180°C).

2  In a bowl, thoroughly combine all of the ingredients from the orange section.

3  Line a baking sheet with parchment paper or a silicone mat—otherwise, everything will stick.

4  Press the mixture over the baking sheet down to a 1 inch (2.5 cm) thickness.

5  If desired, sprinkle with chopped peanuts and peanut butter chips from the blue section.

6  Bake for about 30 minutes.

7  Let cool, then use a pizza cutter to slice into 18 pieces of 1½ × 3 inches (4 × 7.5 cm) each.

8  Does this smell good? No, it smells better than good. It smells like success. Ha! Ha! Ha!

**DID YOU KNOW?**

You can use soy protein powder in place of flour. That's what I've done here!

# The I-Am-Not-a-Pie

*(almond protein pie)*

| Per Serving | |
|---|---|
| Protein | **20 g** |
| Carbohydrates | **22 g** |
| Fiber | **8 g** |

This is a powerful recipe. Whether cooking it in a pie pan, in a springform pan, or on a baking sheet, it is always the perfect snack for the high-performing athlete. Go! Go! Go!

**MAKES** 8 servings, one 9 inch (23 cm) pie
**OVEN TEMPERATURE:** 350°F (180°C)   **COOKING TIME:** 20 minutes

½ cup (150 g) date puree

½ cup (150 g) plain yogurt

1 egg

1 tablespoon (15 ml) pure almond extract

1¼ cups (150 g) soy protein powder

½ cup (50 g) slivered almonds

Slivered almonds, for decoration (optional)

## And then what?

1   Preheat the oven to 350°F (180°C).

2   In a bowl, thoroughly combine all of the ingredients from the orange section. That's it!

3   Line a 9 inch (23 cm) round pie or tart pan with parchment paper or lightly grease—otherwise, everything will stick.

4   Spread the dough into the pan and press down firmly to compress.

5   If desired, sprinkle with the slivered almonds from the blue section.

6   Bake for about 20 minutes.

7   Enjoy the aroma!

8   Use a pizza cutter to slice this treat in a flash.

**TIPSKI!**

For a complete nutritious snack after training, have a piece of fruit along with The I-Am-Not-a-Pie.

**Per Serving***

| | |
|---|---|
| Protein | **3 g** |
| Carbohydrates | **7 g** |
| Fiber | **2 g** |

*Nutritional information calculated using light coconut milk

# The Plump Pom-Pom

*(soy protein, chocolate, and coconut balls)*

If you like crowds cheering you on during a running race, then these Plump Pom-Poms will make you want to outdo yourself.

**MAKES** 28 energy balls, 1 ounce (30 g) each
**OVEN TEMPERATURE:** 350°F (180°C)   **COOKING TIME:** 15 minutes

½ cup (150 g) date puree

1 small can (160 ml) light or regular coconut milk

1 egg

¼ teaspoon (1 ml) ground nutmeg

1 cup (120 g) soy protein powder

½ cup (60 g) coconut flour

¼ cup (25 g) cocoa powder

⅓ cup (33 g) unsweetened shredded coconut

½ cup (100 g) dairy-free chocolate chips of your choice

⅓ cup (33 g) unsweetened shredded coconut, for decoration

## And then what?

1   Preheat the oven to 350°F (180°C).

2   In a bowl, thoroughly combine all of the ingredients from the orange section. The dough should come together into a nice ball.

3   Lightly grease your hands (with vegetable oil, for example) before handling the dough.

4   Divide and roll the dough into 28 small balls. You can flatten them, if you prefer that shape.

5   Roll the balls in the shredded coconut from the blue section to transform them into pom-poms.

6   Line a baking sheet with parchment paper or a silicone mat—otherwise, everything will stick.

7   Transfer the pom-poms onto the prepared baking sheet.

8   Bake for about 15 minutes. Go, go, go!

**TIPSKI!**

**Do you like to snack on these pom-poms every day? Then use light coconut milk.**

**Per Serving**

| | |
|---|---|
| Protein | **2 g** |
| Carbohydrates | **7 g** |
| Fiber | **2 g** |

# The VegaMegaMatcha

*(protein, matcha, and puffed quinoa cookies)*

Naturally vegan and gluten-free, this cookie is a whole mouthful of joy. Simple to prepare, it is sure to sustain you for a long time . . . which is amazing, given how light it is.

**MAKES** 20 energy cookies, 1 ounce (30 g) each

**OVEN TEMPERATURE:** 350°F (180°C)    **COOKING TIME:** 15 to 20 minutes

½ cup (150 g) date puree

1 cup (250 ml) plant-based milk or milk of your choice

⅓ cup (60 g) chia seeds

1 scoop (22 g) vanilla vegan protein powder (I like Vega® Viva Vanilla Protein Smoothie)

1 tablespoon (15 ml) matcha powder

½ cup (25 g) unsweetened toasted coconut flakes

3 cups (60 g) puffed quinoa

## And then what?

1   Preheat the oven to 350°F (180°C).

2   In a bowl, thoroughly combine the ingredients from the orange section.

3   Add the ingredients from the blue section and stir to combine.

4   Line a baking sheet with parchment paper or a silicone mat—otherwise, everything will stick.

5   Drop spoonfuls of dough using a small spoon or cookie scoop to create beautifully round energy cookies.

6   Bake for 15 minutes, or up to 20 minutes if you like crunchy cookies.

7   Let the cookies cool completely before devouring.

8   Move and get a bite of happiness with The VegaMegaMatcha.

### TIPSKI!

Two cookies and a piece of fruit about an hour and a half before training is mega helpful.

| **Per Serving** | |
| --- | --- |
| Protein | **2 g** |
| Carbohydrates | **7 g** |
| Fiber | **1 g** |

# The Suuuuuper Goober

*(plant protein, oat, and peanut cookies)*

Peanut, groundnut, goober . . . there are so many ways to describe this little plant. So much so, that it's almost an Olympic endeavor in itself. Good thing they taste so suuuuuuuuuper.

**MAKES** 20 energy cookies, 1 ounce (30 g) each
**OVEN TEMPERATURE:** 350°F (180°C)   **COOKING TIME:** About 15 minutes

½ cup (150 g) date puree

½ cup (150 g) unsweetened applesauce

½ cup (125 ml) plant-based milk or milk of your choice

2 teaspoons (10 ml) baking powder

1 tablespoon (15 ml) vinegar of your choice

1 scoop (22 g) vanilla vegan protein powder (I like Vega® Viva Vanilla Protein Smoothie)

½ cup (50 g) certified gluten-free quick-cooking oats or rolled oats

½ cup (75 g) chopped peanuts

1 tablespoon (15 ml) chia seeds

## And then what?

1   Preheat the oven to 350°F (180°C).

2   In a bowl, thoroughly combine the ingredients from the orange section.

3   Incorporate the ingredients from the blue section.

4   Line a baking sheet with parchment paper or a silicone mat—otherwise, everything will stick.

5   Drop spoonfuls of dough using a small spoon or cookie scoop to create beautifully round energy cookies.

6   Bake for about 15 minutes.

7   Isn't the smell just suuuuuuuuuper?

**TIPSKI!**

Before your workout, fuel up with two cookies and a piece of fruit. Afterward, enjoy one with Greek yogurt.

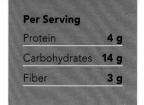

| Per Serving | |
| --- | --- |
| Protein | 4 g |
| Carbohydrates | 14 g |
| Fiber | 3 g |

# The Banana Roll

*(plant protein, banana, and shelled hemp seed cookies)*

Do you like banana bread? This invigorating cookie version is perfect. It's good, it's simple, and you can even eat it for breakfast. With this recipe, there's no need to roll the dice.

**MAKES** 12 energy cookies, 2 ounces (60 g) each
**OVEN TEMPERATURE:** 350°F (180°C)   **COOKING TIME:** 30 minutes

½ cup (150 g) date puree

½ cup (125 ml) plant-based milk or milk of your choice

2 very ripe bananas, mashed with a fork

1 scoop (22 g) vanilla vegan protein powder (I like Vega® Viva Vanilla Protein Smoothie)

2 cups (40 g) puffed quinoa

¼ cup (40 g) chia seeds

¼ cup (35 g) shelled hemp seeds

## And then what?

1   Preheat the oven to 350°F (180°C).
2   In a bowl, thoroughly combine all of the ingredients. That's it!
3   Line a baking sheet with parchment paper or a silicone mat—otherwise, everything will stick.
4   Drop spoonfuls of dough using a small spoon or cookie scoop to create beautifully round energy cookies. Important: make sure to pack the dough when you scoop it.
5   Bake for about 30 minutes.
6   The Banana Roll smells like banana bread. Yummski!

**TIPSKI!**

To maximize your recovery after exercise, eat a serving of fruit along with this cookie.

# 6

# Rousing Biscotti

These treats are crunchy!

# The InFigoring

*(fig, banana, and cinnamon biscotti)*

The first biscotti—or Labriskotti!—to see the light of day.
The InFigoring is perfect for fans of a crunch, pop, and crackle.
Yes, it is fruity and spicy, but what I like most of all is that it's
full of character.

**MAKES** 15 Labriskotti, 1 ounce (30 g) each
**OVEN TEMPERATURE:** 350°F (180°C)  **COOKING TIME:** 1 hour, 20 minutes

½ cup (150 g) date puree

1 cup (250 ml) plant-based milk or
    milk of your choice

1 very ripe banana, mashed with a fork

¼ cup (40 g) chia seeds

½ tablespoon (7 ml) baking powder

¼ to ½ teaspoon (1 to 2 ml) ground
    cinnamon, to taste

Pinch of salt


1 cup (180 g) rustic gluten-free or
    whole wheat bread flour or flour
    of your choice

1 cup (120 g) whole walnuts

½ cup (65 g) raisins

2 cups (110 g) soft dried figs
    (dried, then rehydrated)

## And then what?

1. Preheat the oven to 350°F (180°C).
2. In a bowl, thoroughly combine the ingredients from the orange section.
3. Incorporate the ingredients from the blue section, then mix until the dough is smooth.
4. Gather the dough into a ball in the bottom of the bowl.
5. Line a baking sheet with parchment paper or a silicone mat—otherwise, everything will stick.
6. Lightly oil your hands with vegetable oil. Transfer the dough to the prepared baking sheet, and lightly press down to create a loaf shape.
7. Bake for about 50 minutes. Yay! Smells like energy!
8. Transfer to a cooling rack. Leave the oven on.
9. Slice the loaf into 15 thin Labriskotti, then transfer back to the baking sheet.
10. Bake them for 15 minutes on one side, then flip over and bake for another 15 minutes.
11. Snap—it's so good!

# The Celestial

*(chocolate and pecan biscotti)*

Black, tasty, and filled with divine chocolate, this biscotti
(or Labriskotti!) shines like a constellation. Spread some
pureed dates on top, and you'll launch into orbit. Really!

**MAKES** 15 Labriskotti, 1 ounce (30 g) each
**OVEN TEMPERATURE:** 350°F (180°C)   **COOKING TIME:** 1 hour, 20 minutes

½ cup (150 g) date puree

1 cup (250 ml) plant-based milk or
milk of your choice

¼ cup (75 g) unsweetened applesauce

¼ cup (40 g) chia seeds

1 tablespoon (15 ml) baking powder

Pinch of salt

½ cup (90 g) rustic gluten-free or
whole wheat bread flour or flour
of your choice

½ cup (50 g) cocoa powder

¼ cup (30 g) ground flaxseeds

1 cup (120 g) whole pecans

¾ cup (150 g) dairy-free dark chocolate
chips

## And then what?

1   Preheat the oven to 350°F (180°C).

2   In a bowl, thoroughly combine the ingredients
from the orange section.

3   Incorporate the ingredients from the blue
section, then mix until the dough is smooth.

4   Gather the dough into a ball in the bottom of
the bowl.

5   Line a baking sheet with parchment paper or
a silicone mat—otherwise, everything will stick.

6   Lightly oil your hands with vegetable oil.
Transfer the dough to the prepared baking
sheet, and lightly press down to create a loaf
shape.

7   Bake for about 50 minutes. Yay! Smells like
energy!

8   Transfer to a cooling rack. Leave the oven on.

9   Slice the loaf into 15 thin Labriskotti, then
transfer back to the baking sheet.

10  Bake them for 15 minutes on one side, then
flip over and bake for another 15 minutes.

TIPSKI!

Did you know edible essential oils can be used to flavor your recipes? Give them a try!

# The Lemonette

*(lemon and almond biscotti)*

Fresh. Unique. Summery. I love this yellow lemon Labriskotti.
It's a festival of sunshine and sweets that radiates good health.
Long live The Lemonette!

**MAKES** 15 Labriskotti, 1 ounce (30 g) each
**OVEN TEMPERATURE:** 350°F (180°C)   **COOKING TIME:** 1 hour, 20 minutes

½ cup (150 g) date puree

1 cup (250 ml) plant-based milk or
    milk of your choice

¼ cup (40 g) chia seeds

1 tablespoon (15 ml) baking powder

Grated zest from 1 lemon or 5 drops
    lemon essential oil

Pinch of salt

½ cup (90 g) rustic gluten-free,
    whole wheat bread flour, or flour
    of your choice

½ cup (50 g) almond flour

1 cup (100 g) slivered almonds

¼ cup (50 g) dairy-free white chocolate
    chips (optional)

1 cup (100 g) slivered almonds, for
    garnish

Lemon zest, for garnish

## And then what?

1   Preheat the oven to 350°F (180°C).

2   In a bowl, thoroughly combine the ingredients
    from the orange section.

3   Incorporate the ingredients from the blue
    section, then mix until the dough is smooth.

4   Gather the dough into a ball in the bottom of
    the bowl.

5   Line a baking sheet with parchment paper or
    a silicone mat—otherwise, everything will stick.

6   Lightly oil your hands with vegetable oil.
    Transfer the dough to the prepared baking
    sheet, and lightly press down to create a loaf
    shape. If desired, you can also shape it like a
    lemon!

7   Sprinkle with the chopped slivered almonds
    and some lemon zest from the pink section
    for a stylish touch.

8   Bake for about 50 minutes. Yay! Smells like
    Labriski energy!

9   Transfer to a cooling rack. Leave the oven on.

10  Slice the loaf into 15 thin Labriskotti, then
    transfer back to the baking sheet.

11  Bake them for 15 minutes on one side, then
    flip over and bake for another 15 minutes.

# The Cracker Backer

*(tigernut, hemp seed, and spiced biscotti)*

Surprise! A little bomb of fiber and protein, this cracker is as delicious for breakfast as it is with a bowl of soup.

**MAKES** 18 Labriskotti, 1 ounce (30 g) each
**OVEN TEMPERATURE:** 350°F (180°C)   **COOKING TIME:** 50 minutes

¾ cup (225 g) date puree

1 cup (250 ml) plant-based milk or milk of your choice

1 tablespoon (15 ml) baking powder

¼ teaspoon (1 ml) four-spice blend

Pinch of salt

½ cup (50 g) certified gluten-free oat flour

¼ cup (25 g) tigernut powder

¼ cup (40 g) chia seeds

¼ cup (35 g) shelled hemp seeds

¼ cup (30 g) ground flaxseeds

### DID YOU KNOW?

Rich in fiber, the tigernut is a tuber, not a nut.

## And then what?

1   Preheat the oven to 350°F (180°C).

2   In a bowl, thoroughly combine all of the ingredients.

3   Line a 9 inch (23 cm) round pie or tart pan with parchment paper or lightly grease—otherwise, everything will stick.

4   Spread the dough into the pan and firmly press down.

5   Bake for about 30 minutes. Take the pan out of the oven, and let cool slightly. Leave the oven on.

6   Meanwhile, line a baking sheet with parchment paper.

7   Once the cracker has slightly cooled, transfer to a cutting board and slice into 18 thin slices. Transfer the slices to the prepared baking sheet.

8   Bake them for 10 minutes on one side, then flip over and bake for another 10 minutes.

# The Sunny Bread

*(sunflower seed, rosemary, and turmeric loaf)*

A gourmet loaf? Why, yes . . . with its aroma reminiscent of the Mediterranean, just smelling it is a delight. There's plenty of sun in the bakery!

**MAKES** 1 beautiful loaf, or ½ loaf + 10 Labriskotti    **OVEN TEMPERATURE:** 350°F (180°C)
**COOKING TIME:** 45 minutes + 30 minutes for optional Labriskotti

½ cup (150 g) date puree

1 cup (250 ml) plant-based milk or milk of your choice

1 egg

2 tablespoons (30 ml) baking powder

⅛ teaspoon (0.5 ml) fleur de sel

¼ teaspoon (1 ml) turmeric

2 teaspoons (10 ml) whole dried rosemary leaves

2 cups (300 g) gluten-free flour or flour of your choice

¼ cup (35 g) shelled hemp seeds

¾ cup (105 g) shelled sunflower seeds

1 cup (120 g) mixed sunflower seeds, rosemary, and shelled hemp seeds, for decoration (optional)

## And then what?

1   Preheat the oven to 350°F (180°C).

2   In a bowl, thoroughly combine the ingredients from the orange section.

3   Incorporate the ingredients from the blue section, then stir until the dough is smooth.

4   Gather the dough into a ball in the bottom of the bowl.

5   Line a baking sheet with parchment paper or a silicone mat—otherwise, everything will stick.

6   Lightly oil your hands with vegetable oil. Transfer the dough to the prepared baking sheet, then lightly press down to create a loaf shape.

7   If desired, sprinkle the loaf with the decorating mix from the pink section to create a lovely crust.

8   Bake for about 45 minutes.

9   Transfer to a cooling rack.

10  Yummy, you have bread!

11  You can also slice half of the loaf into 10 thin Labriskotti. Transfer the slices back to the baking sheet and bake them for 15 minutes on one side, then flip over and bake for another 15 minutes. What to do with the other half of the loaf? Eat it like you would bread.

# The Salty and Sweet Deluxe

*(pistachio, pecan, and cranberry or cherry biscotti)*

When salty 'n' sweet meet sour 'n' fruity, you find yourself in a lush world of gourmet possibilities. Dare to try the impossible and take a bite out of life!

**MAKES** 15 Labriskotti, 1 ounce (30 g) each
**OVEN TEMPERATURE:** 350°F (180°C)  **COOKING TIME:** 1 hour, 15 minutes

½ cup (150 g) date puree

1 cup (250 ml) plant-based milk or milk of your choice

1 egg

2 tablespoons (30 ml) baking powder

⅛ teaspoon (0.5 ml) fleur de sel

2 cups (300 g) gluten-free bread flour or flour of your choice

2 tablespoons (30 ml) chia seeds

⅔ cup (80 g) shelled roasted, salted pistachios

⅔ cup (80 g) whole pecans

¾ cup (95 g) dried cranberries or cherries

1 cup (125 g) chopped mixed nuts, for decoration (optional)

## And then what?

1  Preheat the oven to 350°F (180°C).

2  In a bowl, thoroughly combine the ingredients from the orange section.

3  Incorporate the ingredients from the blue section, then mix until the dough is smooth.

4  Gather the dough into a ball in the bottom of the bowl.

5  Line a baking sheet with parchment paper or a silicone mat—otherwise, everything will stick.

6  Lightly oil your hands with vegetable oil. Transfer the dough to the prepared baking sheet, and lightly press down to create a loaf shape.

7  If desired, sprinkle the loaf with the mixed nuts from the pink section to create a luxurious crust.

8  Bake for about 45 minutes.

9  Transfer to a cooling rack. Leave the oven on.

10  Slice the loaf into 15 Labriskotti, then transfer back to the baking sheet.

11  Bake them for 15 minutes on one side, then flip over and bake for another 15 minutes.

TIPSKI!

Try this with cheese.
Yumski!

Date puree
keeps me
going, and
going, and
going . . .
and I know it
will keep you
going too!

# 7

# Inspiring Cakes

Eating healthy is a piece of cake.
(Yes, it really is—believe me.)

# The Royal Colossus

*(quinoa, dates, nuts, and festive pleasures cake)*

Ladies and gentlemen, presenting His Majesty, The Royal Colossus. Treat yourself to something healthy with this dessert worthy of the tables of the greatest royals. Let them eat cake! Oh, yes please.

**MAKES** 6 to 8 servings, one 9 inch (23 cm) round cake
**OVEN TEMPERATURE:** 350°F (180°C)   **COOKING TIME:** 55 minutes

¾ cup (225 g) date puree

¾ cup (225 g) unsweetened applesauce

½ cup (125 ml) plant-based milk or milk of your choice

1 tablespoon (15 ml) baking powder

Pinch of salt

1 cup (120 g) quinoa flour

2½ cups (50 g) puffed quinoa

½ cup (50 g) almond flour

¼ cup (40 g) chia seeds

¼ cup (35 g) shelled hemp seeds

½ to 1 cup (125 to 175 g) whole dates, to taste

1 cup (120 g) whole pecans

1 cup (120 g) whole walnuts

½ cup (100 g) dairy-free dark chocolate chips

½ cup (65 g) dried cranberries sweetened with apple juice

Mixed nuts, for decoration

Pitted dates, for decoration

Chocolate chips, for decoration

Dried cranberries, for decoration

## And then what?

1   Preheat the oven to 350°F (180°C).

2   In a bowl, thoroughly combine the ingredients from the orange section.

3   Incorporate the ingredients from the blue section.

4   Add the ingredients from the pink section.

5   Line a 9 inch (23 cm) tube pan with parchment paper or lightly grease—otherwise, everything will stick.

6   Pour the batter into the pan. Decorate as desired using ingredients from the green section. Don't be light-handed: this is a royal cake, after all!

7   Bake for about 55 minutes.

8   Let cool, then remove from the pan.

### TIPSKI!

Impress your guests by dressing up The Royal Colossus with a beautiful, festive ribbon.

# The Carrot Cake . . . Off!

*(walnut, white chocolate, and carrot cake)*

Why keep cooking like it's the 1950s? Get in your rocket ship and cake off for the 21st century with this energizing, healthy version of the classic carrot cake!

**MAKES** 6 to 8 servings, one 9 inch (23 cm) cake
**OVEN TEMPERATURE:** 350°F (180°C)   **COOKING TIME:** 1 hour, 10 minutes

¾ cup (225 g) date puree

¼ cup (75 g) unsweetened applesauce

1 cup (250 ml) plant-based milk or milk of your choice

2 eggs

1 tablespoon (15 ml) pure vanilla extract

2 teaspoons (10 ml) baking powder

½ teaspoon (2 ml) ground cinnamon

¼ teaspoon (1 ml) ground nutmeg

⅛ teaspoon (0.5 ml) turmeric

Pinch of salt

2 cups (240 g) gluten-free or regular all-purpose flour

2 cups (150 g) peeled, grated carrots

1 cup (120 g) chopped walnuts

⅔ cup (90 g) dried currants

¼ to ½ cup (50 to 100 g) dairy-free white chocolate chips (optional)

Mixed nuts of your choice, for decoration

Raisins of your choice, for decoration

White chocolate chips, for decoration

## And then what?

1   Preheat the oven to 350°F (180°C).

2   In a bowl, thoroughly combine the ingredients from the orange section.

3   Incorporate the ingredients from the blue section.

4   Line a 9 inch (23 cm) tube pan with parchment paper or lightly grease—otherwise, everything will stick.

5   Pour the batter into the pan. Decorate with nuts, raisins, and white chocolate chips from the pink section.

6   Bake for about 1 hour and 10 minutes.

7   You've chosen wisely with this recipe—your house will smell great!

# The Unicorn Dust

*(white cake of your dreams)*

A white cake that tastes like the vanilla cake you buy at the store? That's right! The sprinkles add some sparkle. Kids will find it magical, just magical!

**MAKES** 6 to 8 servings, one 9 inch (23 cm) round cake
**OVEN TEMPERATURE:** 350°F (180°C)   **COOKING TIME:** 30 minutes

¾ cup (225 g) date puree

1 cup (250 ml) plant-based milk or milk of your choice

2 eggs

1½ tablespoons (22 ml) pure vanilla extract

1 tablespoon (15 ml) baking powder

Pinch of salt

1½ cups (225 g) pastry flour

¼ cup (40 g) chia seeds

¼ to ¾ cup (20 to 60 g) rainbow-colored sprinkles, to taste

Rainbow-colored sprinkles, for decoration (optional)

## And then what?

1   Preheat the oven to 350°F (180°C).
2   In a bowl, thoroughly combine all of the ingredients from the orange section. That's it? Yep, it is!
3   Line a 9 inch (23 cm) tube pan with parchment paper or lightly grease—otherwise, everything will stick.
4   Pour the batter into the pan. If desired, decorate with more sprinkles from the blue section.
5   Bake for about 30 minutes.
6   Let cool, remove from the pan, and harvest the bursts of intense joy that erupt out of nowhere. It's official: you're a star!

TIPSKI!

To make sure the sprinkles shine bright, use white flour.

# The Papooski

*(chocolate, caramel, and pecan cake)*

A decadent cake or a healthy dessert? The Papooski is a little bit of both. This creation came into the world to conquer the most skeptical eaters, and it succeeds every time.

**MAKES** 6 to 8 servings, one 8 inch (20 cm) round cake
**OVEN TEMPERATURE:** 350°F (180°C)  **COOKING TIME:** 1 hour

¾ cup (225 g) date puree

½ cup (150 g) unsweetened applesauce

1 cup (250 ml) plant-based milk or milk of your choice

1 egg

1 tablespoon (15 ml) pure vanilla extract or artificial caramel extract

1 tablespoon (15 ml) baking powder

½ teaspoon (2 ml) baking soda

Pinch of salt

1½ cups (225 g) whole wheat pastry flour

½ cup (50 g) cocoa powder

1 cup (120 g) whole pecans

¼ cup (40 g) chia seeds

½ cup (100 g) dairy-free dark chocolate chips

½ cup (80 g) caramel toffee bits or dairy-free caramel chips (optional)

Nuts of your choice, for decoration

Chocolate chips or caramel toffee bits, for decoration

The Healthy Chocolate Sauce (page 187), for serving

## And then what?

1  Preheat the oven to 350°F (180°C).

2  In a bowl, thoroughly combine the ingredients from the orange section.

3  Incorporate the ingredients from the blue section.

4  Add the ingredients from the pink section.

5  Line an 8 inch (20 cm) springform pan with parchment paper or lightly grease—otherwise, everything will stick.

6  Pour the batter into the pan. Decorate with nuts and chocolate chips or caramel toffee bits to impress your guests. Ha! Ha! Ha!

7  Bake for about 1 hour.

8  Meanwhile, prepare The Healthy Chocolate Sauce.

9  To serve, slice the cake and serve with the sauce.

**TIPSKI!**

You can use your favorite gluten-free flour to make this cake gluten-free.

# The Camper's Delirium

*(graham cracker crumb, chocolate, and coconut cake)*

This cake could also be called Deconstructed S'mores. But why deconstruct such a memorable campfire dessert? A bit of delirium is good for morale.

**MAKES** 6 to 8 servings, one 5 × 9 inch (13 × 23 cm) cake
**OVEN TEMPERATURE:** 350°F (180°C)   **COOKING TIME:** 50 minutes

½ cup (150 g) date puree

½ cup (125 ml) plant-based milk or milk of your choice

1 egg

1 tablespoon (15 ml) pure vanilla extract

2 teaspoons (10 ml) baking powder

Pinch of salt

½ cup (60 g) spelt flour or whole wheat flour

1¼ cups (120 g) graham cracker crumbs

¼ cup (40 g) chia seeds

¼ cup (30 g) ground flaxseeds

½ cup (60 g) chopped walnuts

½ cup (50 g) unsweetened shredded coconut

¼ to ½ cup (50 to 100 g) dairy-free dark chocolate chips, to taste

½ to 1 cup (30 to 60 g) marshmallows (optional), to taste

Graham cracker crumbs, for decoration

Chopped nuts, for decoration

Unsweetened shredded coconut, for decoration

Dark chocolate chips, for decoration

## And then what?

1   Preheat the oven to 350°F (180°C).

2   In a bowl, thoroughly combine the ingredients from the orange section.

3   Incorporate the ingredients from the blue section.

4   Line a 5 × 9 inch (13 × 23 cm) loaf pan with parchment paper or lightly grease—otherwise, everything will stick.

5   Pour the batter into the pan. Decorate the cake with graham cracker crumbs, chopped nuts, coconut, and dark chocolate chips from the pink section.

6   Bake for about 50 minutes.

7   Joy! Joy! Joy!

**TIPSKI!**

For a 100% healthy version, just say "So long, marshmallow."

# The Leftovers Are Madeover

*(cake with . . . Easter leftovers)*

A special cake that lets you get creative when your kids get too many chocolates. When they ask, "Where did they go?" you can just say, "I don't know. You must have eaten them all . . ." Ha! Ha!

**MAKES** 6 to 8 servings, one 9 inch (23 cm) round cake
**OVEN TEMPERATURE:** 350°F (180°C)   **COOKING TIME:** 30 minutes

¾ cup (225 g) date puree

1 cup (250 ml) plant-based milk or milk of your choice

2 eggs

1½ tablespoons (22 ml) pure vanilla extract

1 tablespoon (15 ml) baking powder

Pinch of salt

1 cup (150 g) pastry flour

½ cup (50 g) cocoa powder

¼ cup (40 g) chia seeds

Leftover chocolate you want to see disappear!

## And then what?

1   Preheat the oven to 350°F (180°C).

2   In a bowl, thoroughly combine the ingredients from the orange section.

3   Line a 9 inch (23 cm) tube pan with parchment paper or lightly grease—otherwise, everything will stick.

4   Pour half of the batter into the mold, dot with your leftover chocolate pieces, then cover with the rest of the batter.

5   If desired, decorate the top of the cake with additional pieces of chocolate from the blue section.

6   Bake for about 30 minutes.

7   It's going to smell so good in your kitchen!

# The Belle of the Ball

*(orange, rum, and cranberry cake)*

Some people have allergies or food intolerances, while others can (and will) eat just about anything. Your challenge: turning your evening into a great feast. Fortunately, your Belle is ready.

**MAKES** 6 to 8 servings, one 9 inch (23 cm) round cake
**OVEN TEMPERATURE:** 350°F (180°C)   **COOKING TIME:** 50 minutes

⅔ cup (200 g) date puree

¾ cup (180 ml) plant-based milk or milk of your choice

1 tablespoon (15 ml) baking powder

1 tablespoon (15 ml) vinegar of your choice

3 tablespoons (45 ml) spiced rum (optional)

Grated zest from 1 orange or 2 drops orange essential oil

Pinch of salt

½ cup (75 g) chickpea flour

½ cup (60 g) tapioca flour or cornstarch

⅔ cup (70 g) almond flour or tigernut powder

⅔ cup (85 g) dried cranberries sweetened with apple juice

⅔ cup (85 g) dried cherries or (65 g) frozen cranberries

Slivered almonds, for decoration

Dried cranberries, for decoration

Rum, for serving (optional)

## And then what?

1   Preheat the oven to 350°F (180°C).

2   In a bowl, thoroughly combine the ingredients from the orange section.

3   Incorporate the ingredients from the blue section.

4   Line a 9 inch (23 cm) tube pan with parchment paper or lightly grease—otherwise, everything will stick.

5   Pour the dough into the pan. Decorate with slivered almonds and dried cranberries from the pink section. Yummy!

6   Bake for about 50 minutes.

7   Let cool slightly, then remove from the pan.

8   Crazy tip: do you enjoy rum? Using a toothpick, prick some tiny holes into the cake and gently pour a little of this mythical drink into it. Mmm . . .

**TIPSKI!**

Vinegar gives the batter an airiness, but it's undetectable in the finished dessert. No sour taste to worry about!

## MADAME'S MENU

Press mint leaves into a handful of cranberries, and you have decorative mistletoe!

## TIPSKI!

If you use gluten-free flour, this cake will not rise as much, but will be equally delicious.

# The Picky Logger

*(a treat you won't regret come the New Year)*

A Yule log without any added sugar? That's right! Even if you made a New Year's resolution to diet, you don't need to be a picky eater with this! New Year's traditions can still be respected… all in joy and wonder.

**MAKES** 6 to 8 servings, 1 log    **OVEN TEMPERATURE:** 350°F (180°C)    **COOKING TIME:** 14 minutes

¾ cup (225 g) date puree

1 cup (250 ml) plant-based milk or milk of your choice

2 eggs

1½ tablespoons (22 ml) pure vanilla extract

1 tablespoon (15 ml) baking powder

Pinch of salt

1½ cups (225 g) pastry flour or flour of your choice

¼ cup (40 g) chia seeds

⅓ cup (55 g) SKOR caramel toffee bits or dairy-free caramel chips (optional)

The On Duty Ganache (page 187)

The Dark Chocolate Frosting (page 187)

Caramel chips, for decoration (optional)

Unsweetened shredded coconut, for decoration (optional)

## And then what?

1   Preheat the oven to 350°F (180°C).

2   In a bowl, combine all of the log ingredients from the orange section. That's it! Yep, it is!

3   Line a 10 × 15 inch (25 × 38 cm) baking sheet with parchment paper or lightly grease— otherwise, everything will stick.

4   Spread the batter over the baking sheet.

5   Bake for about 14 minutes.

6   Let cool slightly.

7   Place a damp tea towel onto your work surface.

8   Remove the cake from the baking sheet by lifting the parchment paper and turning the cake over onto the kitchen towel. Peel the parchment paper off the cake.

9   Working from the short side of the cake, roll the cake, including the towel, into a log, then let rest until cooled to room temperature.

10  Meanwhile, prepare The On Duty Ganache and The Dark Chocolate Frosting from the blue section.

11  Once the cake is cool, unroll, remove the towel, and spread the ganache all over.

12  Roll into a log again, then cover with the frosting.

13  If desired, decorate with caramel chips and/or shredded coconut from the pink section. Happy Holidays!

# 8

# Amazing Classics

*Amazing classics are good for morale.*

# The Date Barski

*(date, oat, and coconut squares)*

It really exists. A Madame Labriski version of the famous date bar. Or do you like to call it a date square? Whatever the case, I added my own little gourmet touch. Who said classics couldn't be improved?

**MAKES** 9 to 12 squares   **OVEN TEMPERATURE:** 350°F (180°C)   **COOKING TIME:** 40 minutes

3⅔ cups (500 g) pitted dates
1½ cups (375 ml) water

½ cup (150 g) date puree
½ cup (125 ml) soy beverage or milk of your choice
1 egg
2 teaspoons (10 ml) baking powder
Pinch of salt
1 cup (100 g) certified gluten-free oat flour or (120 g) quinoa flour
1 cup (100 g) certified gluten-free quick-cooking oats or quinoa flakes
2 tablespoons (30 ml) chia seeds
2 tablespoons (30 ml) unsweetened shredded coconut
½ cup (60 g) chopped pecans or walnuts

1 tablespoon (15 ml) unsweetened shredded coconut, for decoration
1 tablespoon (15 ml) certified gluten-free rolled oats, for decoration
A few pieces of nuts, for decoration

## And then what?

1   In a saucepan over medium heat, combine the ingredients from the orange section and cook for 10 minutes. Stir and set aside.
2   Preheat the oven to 350°F (180°C).
3   Lightly grease an 8 or 9 inch (20 or 23 cm) square baking dish.
4   In a bowl, combine all the crust ingredients from the blue section.
5   Transfer half of the crust to the prepared dish.
6   Spread the date mixture over the base, then cover with the remaining crust mixture.
7   For an elegant touch, combine the decorative ingredients from the pink section and sprinkle over top.
8   Bake for about 30 minutes.
9   Get ready for a delicious experience!

TIPSKI!

Pecans add crunch and a buttery flavor to this dish.

# The Appleicious Crisp

*(caramel, sunflower seed, and apple crisp)*

How about a healthy version of this comforting fall dessert? You can even make it with fruits picked during a fun family outing!

**MAKES** 6 to 8 servings, one 8 or 9 inch (20 or 23 cm) crisp
**OVEN TEMPERATURE:** 350°F (180°C)   **COOKING TIME:** 30 minutes

6 to 8 cups (550 to 750 g) sliced apples (yep, you can keep the peel on)

2 tablespoons (30 ml) date puree

½ teaspoon (2 ml) ground cinnamon

⅛ teaspoon (0.5 ml) ground nutmeg

1 tablespoon (15 ml) lemon juice

½ cup (150 g) date puree

½ cup (125 ml) plant-based milk or milk of your choice

1 egg

2 teaspoons (10 ml) baking powder

¼ teaspoon (1 ml) ground cinnamon

⅛ teaspoon (0.5 ml) ground nutmeg

Pinch of salt

1 cup (100 g) certified gluten-free oat flour or (120 g) quinoa flour

1 cup (100 g) certified gluten-free quick-cooking oats or quinoa flakes

2 tablespoons (30 ml) chia seeds

⅓ cup (50 g) shelled sunflower seeds

¼ cup (40 g) SKOR caramel toffee bits or dairy-free caramel chips (optional)

## And then what?

1  Preheat the oven to 350°F (180°C).
2  Grease an 8 or 9 inch (20 or 23 cm) square baking dish.
3  In a bowl, combine all the apple ingredients from the orange section.
4  Transfer the mixture to the prepared dish.
5  In a bowl, combine all the crisp ingredients from the blue section, then mix well.
6  Incorporate the ingredients from the pink section.
7  Spread the crisp mixture over the apples.
8  Bake for about 30 minutes.
9  Prepare to make people happy and serve seconds!

### MADAME'S MENU

For an elegant touch, decorate with 1 tablespoon (15 ml) each of sunflower seeds, certified gluten-free rolled oats, and SKOR caramel toffee bits or dairy-free caramel chips before baking!

# The Thrifty Pudding

*(like a pudding)*

A new revolutionary version of the famous pudding from Quebec called *pouding chômeur*—but with no refined sugar. Have you ever noticed that the word "revolution" also includes the word "evolution"? Ha! Ha! Ha! Amazing—just like this dessert.

**MAKES** 6 to 8 servings   **OVEN TEMPERATURE:** 350°F (180°C)   **COOKING TIME:** 50 minutes

1 cup (300 g) date puree
1½ cups (375 ml) plant-based milk or milk of your choice
1 tablespoon (15 ml) pure vanilla extract
2 tablespoons (30 ml) cornstarch

½ cup (150 g) date puree
1 cup (250 ml) plant-based milk or milk of your choice
1½ cups (225 g) pastry flour of your choice
2 teaspoons (10 ml) baking powder
Pinch of salt
2 tablespoons (30 ml) chia seeds

## And then what?

1   Preheat the oven to 350°F (180°C).
2   In a saucepan over medium heat, combine all of the sauce ingredients from the orange section and bring to a simmer. Remove from the heat and let rest.
3   Grease an 8 or 9 inch (20 or 23 cm) square baking dish.
4   In a bowl, combine all of the batter ingredients from the blue section.
5   Transfer the mixture to the prepared dish.
6   Pour the batter into the dish, then cover with the sauce.
7   Bake for about 50 minutes.
8   Even your neighbors will come tell you how delicious this dessert smells! Ha! Ha! Ha!
9   Serve warm or cold. Honey, can I eat some for breakfast? Hmmm . . . yes, you surely can.

# The Yes I Pecan!

*(pecan, date, and caramel pie)*

This delicious treat is inspired by pecan pie. It has no, no, no, refined sugar. And yes, yes, yes, it's scrumptious.

**MAKES** 4 to 6 servings, one 9 inch (23 cm) round pie
**OVEN TEMPERATURE:** 350°F (180°C)   **COOKING TIME:** 30 minutes

⅔ cup (200 g) date puree

⅓ cup (80 ml) plant-based milk or milk of your choice, or cream (15%)

1 teaspoon (5 ml) pure vanilla extract or artificial caramel extract (optional)

2 tablespoons (30 ml) cornstarch

¼ cup (75 g) date puree

1 egg

1 tablespoon (15 ml) cricket powder (optional)

½ cup (50 g) certified gluten-free oat flour

1 cup (100 g) certified gluten-free quick-cooking oats

2 tablespoons (30 ml) chia seeds

1 cup (120 g) whole pecans, for decoration

⅓ cup (40 g) walnuts, for decoration

2 tablespoons (30 ml) SKOR caramel toffee bits or dairy-free caramel chips, for decoration (optional)

## And then what?

1   In a saucepan over low heat, combine the first three ingredients from the orange section. When the mixture simmers, whisk in the cornstarch. Cover and set aside so it stays warm.

2   Preheat the oven to 350°F (180°C).

3   In a bowl, combine all the base ingredients from the blue section.

4   Line a 9 inch (23 cm) round pie or tart pan with parchment paper or lightly grease—otherwise, everything will stick.

5   Spread the base mixture over the bottom of the pan.

6   Cover with the date mixture, then decorate with the ingredients from the pink section.

7   Bake for about 30 minutes.

8   Does it look like pecan pie? Yes. Is it pecan pie? Yes—without the sugar! Ha! Ha! Ha!

### DID YOU KNOW?

This recipe can be made with other nuts! That's nuts.

# The Appeeling Apple Pie

*(apple, caramel, and coconut pie)*

Evolution is everywhere with this version of the *tarte tatin* (upside-down apple pie). Since I like to keep things simple, I even leave the peels on the apples. Fascinating and magical! That's an appeeling apple pie. Ha! Ha! Ha!

**MAKES** 4 to 6 servings, one 9 inch (23 cm) round pie
**OVEN TEMPERATURE:** 350°F (180°C)  **COOKING TIME:** 10 to 15 minutes + 50 minutes

1 tablespoon (15 ml) olive oil

1⅓ pounds (600 g) large apples, sliced in half (4 to 6 apples—yes, you can leave the peels on!)

¼ cup (75 g) date puree

1 small can (160 ml) light or regular coconut milk

½ tablespoon (7 ml) artificial caramel extract

2 teaspoons (10 ml) cornstarch

½ cup (150 g) date puree

½ cup (150 g) unsweetened applesauce

1 egg

1 tablespoon (15 ml) baking powder

Pinch of salt

½ cup (60 g) gluten-free all-purpose flour or flour of your choice

½ cup (50 g) almond flour

¼ cup (30 g) coconut flour

1 tablespoon (15 ml) SKOR caramel toffee bits or dairy-free caramel chips, for decoration (optional)

¼ cup (30 g) chopped walnuts, for decoration (optional)

## And then what?

1  Preheat the oven to 350°F (180°C).

2  Warm up the oil from the orange section in a skillet over medium heat.

3  Add the rest of the ingredients from the orange section, then cook for 10 to 15 minutes.

4  Meanwhile, prepare the crust by combining all of the ingredients from the blue section in a bowl.

5  Lightly grease a 9 inch (23 cm) pie pan.

6  Transfer the apple mixture to the prepared pie pan, then add the ingredients from the pink section, if desired.

7  Spread the crust mixture over the apples.

8  Bake for about 50 minutes.

9  To serve, set a large plate over the skillet and flip it over to remove it from the pan.

10  Fascinating and magical!

# The Fairy-of-the-Fields

*(fruit pie)*

This is a fruit pie that can hold its own. The epitome of fruity perfection, as seen in Hollywood films. Nothing falling off. No mess. Did a fairy create this?

**MAKES** 4 to 6 servings, one 9 inch (23 cm) round pie
**OVEN TEMPERATURE:** 350°F (180°C)   **COOKING TIME:** 42 minutes

⅓ cup (100 g) date puree
1⅓ cups (160 g) graham cracker crumbs

3 cups (420 g) mixed frozen berries (raspberries, blueberries, strawberries)
½ cup (150 g) date puree

2 tablespoons (30 ml) cornstarch
½ packet (3.5 g) powdered gelatin or 4 g agar-agar

### TIPSKI!

The biggest challenge in this recipe is to make a beautiful crust. Take your time. You can do this.

## And then what?

1   Preheat the oven to 350°F (180°C).
2   In a bowl, prepare the graham cracker crust by combining all the ingredients from the orange section.
3   Line a 9 inch (23 cm) round pie or tart pan with parchment paper or lightly grease—otherwise, everything will stick.
4   Spread the graham cracker mixture over the bottom of the prepared pan, then press it down. Set aside.
5   Your challenge: resisting the urge to taste the mixture at this point!
6   Prepare the filling. In a saucepan, combine the ingredients from the blue section. Set over medium heat, then cook for 12 minutes, or until the fruits are very soft and start to break down.
7   Remove from the heat, then stir in the ingredients from the pink section.
8   Pour the fruit mixture into the prepared crust.
9   Bake for 30 minutes.
10  The sweet scent of The Fairy-of-the-Fields . . . will invade your kitchen.

# The Oven Do-Nuts

*(plain donuts)*

Fried donuts? Not here. These donuts are baked in a donut mold. Look at how happy this round shape with a hole in the middle makes us! Invest in this mold and you will become a millionaire . . . in smiles from ear to ear.

**MAKES** 10 to 12 donuts, about 2 ounces (60 g) each
**OVEN TEMPERATURE:** 350°F (180°C)   **COOKING TIME:** 15 minutes

½ cup (150 g) date puree

1 (155 g) small can coconut milk

2 eggs

1 tablespoon baking powder

¼ teaspoon (1 ml) ground nutmeg

Pinch of salt

1½ cups (180 g) pastry flour

Decorations of your choice (such as unsweetened shredded coconut or chopped nuts) (optional)

### And then what?

1   Preheat the oven to 350°F (180°C).
2   In a bowl, thoroughly combine all of the ingredients from the orange section.
3   Lightly grease the donut pan—otherwise, everything will stick.
4   Fill the donut cups three-quarters of the way up (the donuts will puff up upon baking!).
5   Bake for about 15 minutes.
6   Let cool, then remove from the pan.
7   If desired, decorate the donuts with ingredients from the blue section, then make another batch.
8   The smell will be memorable and the texture . . . sooo soft. Enjoy!

**TIPSKI!**

Feeling fancy? Dip the donuts in one of The Divine Delights (page 187) or slather with one of The Madness Spreads (page 17).

# The Velvety Delight

*(like a cream pie)*

There's no added sugar, and yet kids ask for this again and again.
It's a favorite go-to dessert recipe.

**MAKES** 4 servings, ½ cup (125 ml) each
**STOVETOP TEMPERATURE:** Medium heat   **COOKING TIME:** About 10 minutes

⅓ cup (100 g) date puree

4 egg yolks

¼ cup (30 g) cornstarch

1 tablespoon (15 ml) pure vanilla extract or artificial caramel extract (optional)

½ cup (125 ml) plant-based milk or milk of your choice

⅓ cup (40 g) chopped pecans, for decoration

⅓ cup (55 g) SKOR caramel toffee bits or dairy-free caramel chips, for decoration

Sliced fresh banana or banana chips, for decoration

## And then what?

1   In a bowl, combine the ingredients from the orange section.

2   In a saucepan over medium heat, warm up the milk from the blue section.

3   As soon as it starts simmering, vigorously whisk in the date puree mixture.

4   Simmer for a short time . . . until the mixture thickens.

5   Pour the mixture into a square 8 inch (20 cm) pan.

6   To make it even better, top with the ingredients from the pink section. Have fun!

7   Cover and refrigerate.

8   Serve in small bowls.

9   A mountain of compliments is waiting for you when you share this recipe with those you love. Go grab them!

**TIPSKI!**

You can add a layer of The Velvety Delight in between two layers of cake. It's perfection!

# The Velvety Sparkle

*(like a chocolate and mint–flavored pudding)*

Who doesn't like mint chocolate? Don't resist; just treat yourself to this pleasure.

**MAKES** 4 servings, ½ cup (125 ml) each
**STOVETOP TEMPERATURE:** Medium heat   **COOKING TIME:** About 10 minutes

⅓ cup (100 g) date puree
4 egg yolks
¼ cup (40 g) cornstarch
2 teaspoons (10 ml) pure mint or peppermint extract

½ cup (125 ml) plant-based milk or milk of your choice
¼ cup (25 g) cocoa powder

⅓ cup (65 g) dairy-free dark chocolate chips

Small fresh mint leaves, for decoration (optional)
Small handful blueberries, for decoration (optional)
Sifted cocoa powder, for decoration (optional)

## And then what?

1   In a bowl, combine the ingredients from the orange section.
2   In a saucepan, whisk the ingredients from the blue section over medium heat.
3   As soon as it starts simmering, vigorously whisk in the date puree mixture.
4   Whisk in the dark chocolate chips from the pink section and cook for a short time . . . until the mixture thickens.
5   Pour evenly among four small dessert cups. Cover and refrigerate.
6   To serve, decorate with desired ingredients from the green section.
7   Get ready, mint chocolate fans will be thrilled!

# The Cupid's Clouds

*(like a soft meringue)*

This recipe is light—so light—and just sweet enough. Is it like meringue? I'd rather say it's like a cloud: soft and fluffy . . . with a little taste of heaven.

**MAKES** 35 servings, $\frac{1}{10}$ ounce (3 g) each
**OVEN TEMPERATURE:** 100°F (38°C)  **COOKING TIME:** 2 hours, 30 minutes

½ cup (150 g) date puree
½ cup (125 ml) plant-based milk or milk of your choice
1 tablespoon (15 ml) pure vanilla, almond, or mint extract (optional)

½ cup (125 ml) liquid egg whites (4 egg whites)

1 tablespoon (15 ml) cornstarch

### TIPSKI!

Store these clouds at room temperature in an airtight container. They're best enjoyed within 36 hours.

## And then what?

1  Preheat the oven to 100°F (38°C).
2  In a saucepan over medium-low heat, stir together all the ingredients from the orange section, bring to a low simmer, and set aside.
3  Meanwhile, beat the egg whites from the blue section using a hand mixer.
4  When the egg whites form peaks, gently incorporate the mixture from the orange section.
5  Beat in the cornstarch from the pink section. The mixture should be stiff.
6  Line a baking sheet with parchment paper or lightly grease—otherwise, everything will stick.
7  Drop dollops of "snow" on the prepared baking sheet using a small spoon or a cookie scoop.
8  The snow will turn into clouds after baking for 2 hours and 30 minutes.
9  Oh, my goodness . . . they're just so impressive. Make these and I promise they won't even last an hour.

# The Ciao Ciao Marshmallow

*(like marshmallow-free puffed rice squares)*

No, no, no, no, no! Yes, yes, yes, yes, yes. Is there anything else to add? There's so much you can do with date puree . . . like make these puffed rice squares and oh so much else! Muchas gracias!

**MAKES** 16 squares, 2 inches (5 cm) each
**STOVETOP TEMPERATURE:** Medium heat   **REFRIGERATION TIME:** 1 hour

⅓ cup (100 g) date puree

4 egg yolks

¼ cup (40 g) cornstarch

1 tablespoon (15 ml) pure vanilla extract or artificial caramel extract (optional)

½ cup (125 ml) plant-based milk or milk of your choice

6 cups (540 g) crispy rice cereal

¼ cup (40 g) chia seeds

⅓ cup (55 g) SKOR caramel toffee bits or dairy-free caramel chips (optional)

## And then what?

1 In a bowl, combine the ingredients from the orange section.

2 In a saucepan over medium heat, warm up the milk from the blue section.

3 As soon as it starts simmering, vigorously whisk in the date puree mixture.

4 Simmer for a short time . . . until the mixture thickens.

5 Mix in the ingredients from the pink section.

6 Lightly grease a square 8 inch (20 cm) baking pan—otherwise, everything will stick.

7 Transfer the mixture to the prepared pan and press down firmly.

8 Refrigerate for at least 1 hour.

9 To serve, slice into squares or triangles.

10 You'll need to eat these immediately . . . or at least within 48 hours.

### TIPSKI!

Mix in 1 tablespoon (15 ml) matcha powder and substitute caramel chips with dairy-free white chocolate chips for another tasty treat.

# The Truffleskis

*(date and cocoa truffles)*

Have you ever tasted a delicious chocolate treat that elicited happiness, joy, love, and peace in just one bite? Well, get ready. That's what these truffles (or Truffleskis!) will do. You can serve your guests a Truffleski as a palate cleanser. Ha! Ha! Ha! What's more, they are easy to make. There is no cooking time required! Yipee!

**MAKES** 20 truffles

½ cup (150 g) date puree
⅓ cup (35 g) cocoa powder

¼ cup (25 g) cocoa powder

**Suggested Decorations:**
**Ground pecans**
**Unsweetened shredded coconut**
**Ground almonds**
**Matcha powder**
**Multicolored sprinkles**

### And then what?

1 In a large bowl, combine the ingredients from the orange section. Warning: the cocoa powder may puff up.
2 Stir until the mixture is smooth.
3 Lightly grease your hands with vegetable oil, then roll the mixture into 20 small balls.
4 Roll the balls in cocoa powder from the blue section or, if desired, the decorations listed in the pink section.

## TIPSKI!

The truffles can be stored in an airtight container in the refrigerator for up to 3 days or in the freezer.

# The Saucy Cranberry

*(like a cranberry sauce)*

Oh, small festive red fruit, you have so many nicknames: foxberry, lingonberry, cranberry . . . it's all the same in this delicious sauce, which is simply perfect for a certain turkey holiday!

**MAKES** 1½ cups (375 ml)   **STOVETOP TEMPERATURE:** Medium heat
**COOKING TIME:** 15 minutes

½ cup (150 g) date puree
**4 cups (400 g) frozen cranberries**
½ teaspoon (2 ml) ground cinnamon

## And then what?

1   In a saucepan, combine all of the ingredients.
2   Simmer over medium heat for 15 minutes, stirring from time to time.
3   Great! Finally, a cranberry sauce that's not too sweet and just tart enough.
4   The sauce will keep in the refrigerator for up to 5 days.

### TIPSKI!

You can enjoy The Saucy Cranberry as a condiment for turkey and pork . . . but also as a delicious filling in a muffin! See The My Heart Belongs to You Cranberry on page 83.

# The Strawberry Thingy

*(half jam, half coulis)*

It's not really a jam or a sauce. It's . . . different. Both lighter and fresher, it's great on cakes, bread, yogurt, ice cream . . . it's just about perfect. It's, you know, a thingy . . . a strawberry thingy!

**MAKES** 1½ cups (375 ml)   **STOVETOP TEMPERATURE:** Medium heat
**COOKING TIME:** 10 minutes

⅓ cup (100 g) date puree
4 cups (560 g) frozen strawberries
2 tablespoons (30 ml) lemon juice
3 tablespoons (45 ml) chia seeds

1 tablespoon (2 g) agar-agar or
   2 tablespoons (30 ml) liquid pectin

## And then what?

1   In a saucepan, combine the ingredients from the orange section.

2   Simmer over medium heat for 10 minutes, stirring from time to time.

3   Add the ingredient of your choice from the blue section.

4   Transfer to one or two jars, then refrigerate. This will keep in the refrigerator for up to 5 days.

5   Easy, no? Yes!

**TIPSKI!**

Craving a strawberry pie? Just add 2 tablespoons (30 ml) cornstarch and ½ packet (3.5 g) powdered gelatin or 4 g agar-agar in place of the blue section. Yummy!

# The Divine Delights: Sauce, Frosting, and Ganache

Making healthy choices is part of life. These delights taste like *joie de vivre*, and they give us energy. What more could you want? Indulge in these divine delights and tell me what you think! Can you resist the temptation to eat them all by the spoonful? I can't!